Enchanted Rendezvous: John C. Houbolt and the Genesis of the Lunar-Orbit Rendezvous Concept

by James R. Hansen

NASA History Office
Code ZH
Office of Policy and Plans
NASA Headquarters
Washington, DC 20546

Monographs in Aerospace History Series #4
Reprinted January 1999

Foreword

One of the most critical technical decisions made during the conduct of Project Apollo was the method of flying to the Moon, landing on the surface, and returning to Earth. Within NASA during this debate several modes emerged. The one eventually chosen was lunar-orbit rendezvous (LOR), a proposal to send the entire lunar spacecraft up in one launch. It would head to the Moon, enter into orbit, and dispatch a small lander to the lunar surface. It was the simplest of the various methods, both in terms of development and operational costs, but it was risky. Since rendezvous would take place in lunar, instead of Earth, orbit there was no room for error or the crew could not get home. Moreover, some of the trickiest course corrections and maneuvers had to be done after the spacecraft had been committed to a circumlunar flight.

Between the time of NASA's conceptualization of the lunar landing program and the decision in favor of LOR in 1962, a debate raged between advocates of the various methods. John C. Houbolt, an engineer at the Langley Research Center in Hampton, Virginia, was one of the most vocal of those supporting LOR and his campaign in 1961 and 1962 helped to shape the deliberations in a fundamental way. The monograph that is printed here is an important contribution to the study of NASA history in general, and the process of accomplishing a large-scale technological program (in this case Apollo) in particular. In many ways, the lunar mode decision was an example of heterogeneous engineering, a process that recognizes that technological issues are also simultaneously organizational, economic, social, and political. Various interests often clash in the decision-making process as difficult calculations have to be made and decisions taken. What perhaps should be suggested is that a complex web or system of ties between various people, institutions, and interests brought forward the lunar-orbit rendezvous mode of going to the Moon in the 1960s.

This is the fourth publication in a new series of special studies prepared by the NASA History Office. The **Monographs in Aerospace History** series is designed to provide a wide variety of investigations relative to the history of aeronautics and space. These publications are intended to be focused tightly in terms of subject, relatively short in length, and reproduced in an inexpensive format to allow timely and broad dissemination to researchers in aerospace history. Suggestions for additional publications in the **Monographs in Aerospace History** series are welcome.

Originally printed in November 1995, this Monograph was very popular and went out of print. The NASA History Office is reprinting this Monograph with the original text, two slightly different photos, and some other very minor layout changes. We hope you find the LOR story engaging and especially timely in light of the thirtieth anniversary of the Apollo 11 mission in July 1999.

Roger D. Launius
Chief Historian
National Aeronautics and Space Administration
15 December 1998

There was a reluctance to believe that the rendezvous maneuver was an easy thing. In fact, to a layman, if you were to explain what you had to do to perform a rendezvous in space, he would say that sounds so difficult we'll never be able to do it this century.

Clinton E. Brown, head, Langley Lunar Mission Steering Group on Trajectories and Guidance (from an interview with the author, 17 July 1989)

I'm not so sure we ever thought of rendezvous as very complicated. It's an amazing thing. We thought that if our guys could work out the orbital mechanics and we gave the pilot the right controls and stuff, then he'd land it and make the rendezvous. We didn't think it was very complicated.

Arthur W. Vogeley, Langley Guidance and Control Branch (from an interview with the author, 17 July 1989)

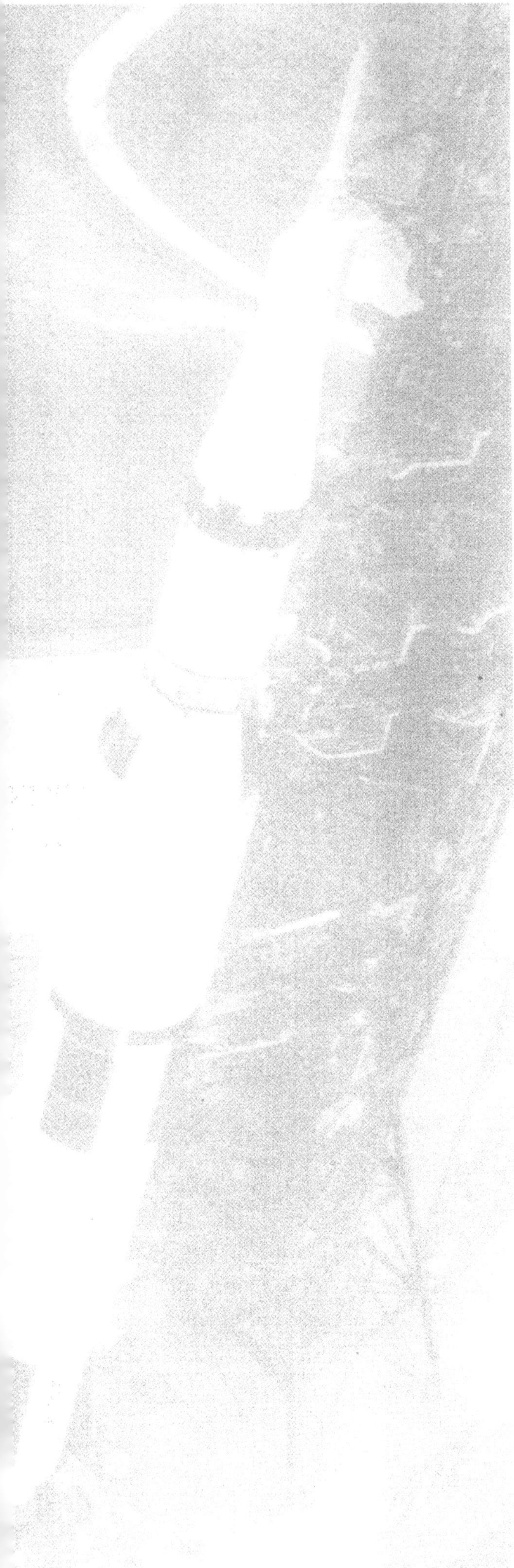

Table of Contents

Introduction

On Thursday morning, 25 May 1961, in a speech to a joint session of Congress, President John F. Kennedy challenged Americans to rebound from their recent second-place finishes in the space race. "First, I believe that this nation should commit itself to achieving the goal, before this decade is out, of landing a man on the moon and returning him safely to earth. No single space project . . . will be more exciting, or more impressive . . . or more important . . . and none will be so difficult or expensive." The dynamic 43-year-old president also told the American people, "It will not be one man going to the Moon, it will be an entire nation. For all of us must work to put him there."[1]

At first, no one at NASA's Langley Research Center in Hampton, Virginia, could quite believe it. If President Kennedy had in fact just dedicated the country to lunar landing, he could not be serious about doing it in less than nine years. It was just not possible. NASA had been studying the feasibility of different lunar missions for some time. But sending an astronaut—one that landed on and returned from the surface of the Moon safely by the end of the 1960s? NASA was not exactly sure how that lunar mission could be accomplished at all, let alone achieved in so little time.

Not even Robert R. Gilruth, the leader of the Space Task Group (STG) located at Langley and the long-standing site of spacecraft expertise in the young federal agency, was prepared for the sensational announcement. When he heard the news, he was in a NASA airplane somewhere over the Midwest on his way to a meeting in Tulsa. He knew that Kennedy planned to say something dramatic about the space program in his speech, and he asked the pilot to patch it through live on the radio. Looking out the window over the passing clouds, he heard every word and was struck by the incredible goal.

President John F. Kennedy addressing a joint session of Congress on 25 May 1961 to announce an accelerated lunar landing program. ***NASA #70-H-1075***

The message stunned him. "An accelerated program, yes," he wanted that. "A lunar landing, yes, in an orderly fashion, with time to work through all the difficulties that such an enterprise was bound to encounter," he wanted that, too. "But not this," he thought to himself.[2] This was too much, too fast. Talk about overconfidence—the first piloted Mercury flight by Alan Shepard had taken place only three weeks ago, on 5 May; NASA had made this one brief fifteen-minute suborbital flight—not even a complete orbit yet—and the president announced that the nation is going to the Moon and on a very ambitious schedule. Suddenly, the STG really had more than it could handle. It already was busy preparing for another suborbital flight (Virgil I. "Gus" Grissom's, on 21 July 1961) and for the first orbital flight sometime early next year (John Glenn's, on 20 February 1962). The group's top talent was still "involved almost exclusively" preparing for the first American orbital flight, and Gilruth himself, before the president's announcement, "had spent almost no time at all" on lunar studies, so demanding were the activities of Project Mercury.[3]

Only one word described Gilruth's feelings at that moment: "aghast." Aghast at the audacity of the president's goal: for American astronauts to fly a quarter of a million miles, make a pinpoint landing on a familiar but yet so strange heavenly body, blast off, and return home safely after a voyage of several days through space—all this by the end of the decade. Only one thought was more daunting, and that was that he was one of the people who would have to make it happen.

But only the project managers directly responsible for making Mercury a success felt so burdened in 1961 by the prospects of having to meet the lunar commitment. Other planners and dreamers about space exploration inside NASA, whose natural curiosity and professional inclination led to speculation about the profiles of future missions, were elated.

For example, inside the small Theoretical Mechanics Division set up inside the old stability wind tunnel building at NASA Langley, Clinton E. Brown and his mathematically oriented colleagues, having heard about Kennedy's announcement, said, "Hooray, let's put on full speed ahead, and do what we can." In their minds, landing astronauts on the Moon as quickly as possible was obviously the right thing to do next if the United States was going to win the "space race." Moreover, Brown and his team—plus one other key Langley researcher, Dr. John C. Houbolt, a rendezvous expert not part of Brown's group, who later became the leading actor in the lunar-orbit rendezvous drama—were confident that they had figured out the best way to accomplish it some time ago.[4] To understand this confidence, however, an understanding of earlier developments provides necessary context.

Brown's Lunar Exploration Working Group

In Sputnik's wake in late 1957, a small circle of Langley researchers had plunged into the dark and frigid depths of space science. "We were aeronautical engineers," remembers William H. Michael, Jr., a member of Clinton E. Brown's Theoretical Mechanics Division who had just returned to Langley after a two-year stint in the aircraft industry. "We knew how to navigate in the air, but we didn't know a thing about orbital mechanics, celestial trajectories, or interplanetary travel, so we had to teach ourselves the subjects." In the Langley technical library, where during the days of the National Advisory Committee for Aeronautics (NACA) the word "space" was not even allowed, Michael could find only one book that helped. It was *An Introduction to Celestial Mechanics* but it had been published in 1914, before the first pioneering rocketry had taken place under Robert H. Goddard. Michael had never heard of its author, a British professor of astrophysics named Forrest R. Moulton.[5] With this out-of-date text in hand, nevertheless, Michael and a few associates taught themselves enough about the equations of celestial mechanics to grow confident in their computations. Before long, the novices had transformed themselves into experts and were using their slide rules and early electronic computers to figure out ways to reach the Moon and to return.

This team did not know at the time how useful their calculations would so quickly turn out to be. In anticipating the trajectories for different lunar missions in the late 1950s, Brown, Michael, and their colleagues were "leapfrogging" over what most people deemed "the logical next step": an Earth-orbiting "space station." The group also did not know that their mental gymnastics would set the direction of the U.S. space program for the next twenty years.

Even after Sputnik, most proponents of space travel still believed—following the wisdom of Konstantin Tsiolkovskiy, Hermann Oberth, Guido von Pirquet, Wernher von Braun, and other space-minded visionaries—that humankind's first step out into the universe would be to some sort of space station in the Earth's orbit. From this nearby outpost, which could also serve as a research laboratory in which all sorts of unique experiments and valuable industrial enterprises might be conducted, human travelers could eventually venture out in spaceships for trips to the Moon, the planets, and beyond. Therefore, after establishing Project Mercury, and putting an astronaut into space, most in NASA believed that the development of a space station was "the next logical step." It was the perfect target project by which NASA could focus its space-related studies as well as its future plans.[6]

But Clint Brown and his associates felt differently: the politics of the space race were dictating the terms of the American space program, not the inspired prophecies of the earliest space pioneers. The Soviet Union had already demonstrated that it had larger boosters than did the United States, which meant that the Soviets had the capability of establishing a space station before Americans could do so. Brown explained years later, "If we put all our efforts into putting a space station around the world, we'd probably find ourselves coming in second again." The "obvious answer" was that "you had to take a larger bite and decide what can really give us leadership in the space race." To him "that clearly seemed the possibility of going to the Moon and landing there."[7] In other words, what Brown was arguing, in this feverish and confused early stage of the spaceflight revolution, was that the "obvious answer" should take precedence over the "next logical step."

The conviction inside Brown's Theoretical Mechanics Division in favor of lunar studies over space station studies grew stronger in early 1959, when Langley's Associate Director, Eugene Draley, agreed to form a Langley working group to study the problems of lunar exploration. Brown, the catalytic group leader, asked for the participation of six of Langley's most thoughtful analysts: David Adamson, Supersonic Aerodynamics Division; Paul R. Hill, Pilotless Aircraft Research Division; John C. Houbolt, Dynamic Loads Division; Albert A. Schy, Stability Research Division; Samuel Katzoff, Full-Scale Research Division; and Bill Michael of Brown's Theoretical Mechanics Division. Dr. Leonard Roberts, a talented young mathematician from England, eventually joined the group. Brown assembled them for the first time in late March 1959 and then periodically into 1960. Besides advising Langley management on the establishment of lunar-related research programs, Brown's people also organized a course in space mechanics for interested center employees. For many involved, this course offered their first real exposure to relativity theory. The Brown study group even disseminated information about the Moon by holding public seminars led by experts from Langley and nearby universities.[8]

Everything about this original lunar study group was done quietly and without much fuss. In those early days of NASA, when the management of research was still loose and did not always require formal research authorizations or approval from NASA headquarters in Washington, the research center pretty much ran itself. Langley management, from Director Henry Reid and Associate Director Floyd Thompson on down, was oriented toward research and encouraged its people to take some initiative. When Brown expressed his desire to work more on lunar exploration than on the space station, Draley simply told him, "Fine, go ahead." Henceforth, he and his lunar working group accentuated their efforts in studying the problems associated with how America would someday reach the Moon. They were doing what Langley researchers did best: they were exploring an interesting new idea and seeing how far they could go with it.

The researchers at Langley were not the only Americans thinking seriously about lunar missions. There were officers in the Air Force, people in "think tanks," professors at universities, and other engineers and scientists in and around NASA all contemplating going to the Moon. In February 1959, a month before the creation of Brown's lunar exploration group at Langley, NASA headquarters created a small Working Group on Lunar and Planetary Surfaces Exploration. (This later evolved into the Science Committee on Lunar Exploration.) Chaired by Dr. Robert Jastrow, the head of NASA headquarters' new Theoretical Division, the working group included such leaders in planetology and lunar science as Harold C. Urey, professor at large at the University of California at San Diego, as well as a number of leading scientists from the Jet Propulsion Laboratory in Pasadena, California, and a few from Langley. In their meetings, Jastrow's group looked into the chances for both a "rough" landing on the Moon—wherein a probe would crash into the surface and be destroyed but not until an on-board camera sent back dozens of valuable pictures to the Earth—as well as "soft" landings wherein a spacecraft would actually land intact on the Moon. Langley's William Michael attended one of the first meetings of Jastrow's committee. Partly in reaction to what he had heard at this meeting, Michael and others at Langley began developing some ideas for photographic reconnaissance of the Moon's surface from lunar orbit, as well as for lunar impact studies.[9] John Houbolt, of Langley's Dynamic Loads Division, also participated in some of these meetings to share his knowledge of the requirements for spacecraft rendezvous.

Two months later, in April 1959, NASA headquarters formed a Research Steering Committee on Manned Space Flight. The purpose of this special committee—which was chaired by former Langley engineer Harry J. Goett, the first Director of NASA's Goddard Space Flight Center—was to analyze human-in-space problems, make recommendations about the missions to follow Project Mercury, and to explore the technological "stepping stones" necessary to prepare for future missions. It would then set forth the general outline of research programs to support those missions.[10]

In its final report, which appeared at the end of 1959, the Goett Committee (as it was known) called for a lunar landing with astronauts as the appropriate long-term goal of NASA's space program. But between the present emphasis on Project Mercury and that goal, there needed to be major interim programs designed to develop advanced orbital capabilities and a manned space station.

Langley's representative on the Goett Committee, Laurence K. Loftin, Jr., the technical assistant to Langley Research Center Associate Director Floyd L. Thompson, agreed with this thinking. However, two other members, the STG's Max Faget and George M. Low, NASA's Director of Spacecraft and Flight Missions in Washington, did not. During meetings from May to December 1959, they voiced the minority opinion: that the Moon should be NASA's next objective after Mercury. George Low, brought to NASA headquarters by Director of Space Flight Programs Abe Silverstein from NASA's Lewis Research Center in Cleveland, was particularly vocal. Not only did Low want to go to the Moon, he wanted Americans to land on it, and as soon as possible.[11]

Michael's Paper on a "Parking Orbit"

Meanwhile at Langley, members of Brown's lunar exploration group were already studying ways for landing on the Moon someday. They explored several options and ideas, but in one of these studies, by Bill Michael, the group examined the benefits of "parking" the Earth-return propulsion portion of a spacecraft in orbit around the Moon during a landing mission.

The spark for Michael's interest in what eventually was called a "parking orbit," a spacecraft in a "waiting" orbit around the Moon or some other celestial body, involved his own calculations to determine whether there was any advantage in a lunar mission to some additional "staging." Staging was a proven and necessary technological concept, first explained by Tsarist Russia's space visionary Tsiolkovskiy in the late 1800s, by which a self-propelled, staged-rocket vehicle (Tsiolkovskiy called it a rocket "train") could ascend to greater and greater heights as its different stages expended their fuel and separated.

In a lunar landing mission, Michael speculated, one would not want to fly a big rocket directly from the Earth to the Moon, as Jules Verne's popular book and other science fiction fantasies envisioned. The big rocket would result in too much unnecessary weight being taken down to the surface. It would be much wiser to take "an intermediate step" and go into lunar orbit, where much of the total weight remained behind—the structure of the interplanetary spacecraft, its heavy fuel load for leaving lunar orbit and heading home, and its massive heat shield necessary for a safe reentry into the Earth's atmosphere. "It's very expensive to accelerate any type of mass to high velocity," Michael reasoned. "Any time you do not have to do that, you save a lot of fuel and thus a lot of weight."[12]

The upshot of his calculations, which he documented in early 1960 in a never-to-be-published paper titled, "Weight Advantages of Use of Parking Orbit for Lunar Soft Landing Mission," was to identify one of the most basic advantages of what eventually was known as the concept of "lunar-orbit rendezvous." Michael had to make several assumptions about what might entail a lunar landing mission—the spacecraft's engines, the structural weights, and so forth. But his results implied that by going into orbit around the Moon rather than going directly to the lunar surface, one could save an impressive 50 percent or more of the total mission weight. Figuring the numbers did not require any difficult or sophisticated calculations.[13] Nor did it require any knowledge of the writings of Russian rocket theoretician Yuri Kondratyuk and British scientist and Interplanetary Society member H.E. Ross, both of whom had expressed the fundamentals of the lunar-orbit rendezvous concept (Kondratyuk in 1916 and Ross in 1948).[14] Neither Michael nor anyone else at Langley at this point, so they have always maintained, had any knowledge of those precursors.

The Langley scientists also had not yet known anything about competition from contemporaries. That did not take long, however. Later the same morning that Michael first presented his rough "parking orbit" calculations in Clint Brown's office, a team led by Thomas E. Dolan from Vought Astronautics, a division of the Chance-Vought Corporation in Dallas, gave a briefing at Langley. This briefing concerned Vought's ongoing company-funded, confidential study of different problems related to "Manned Lunar Landing and Return" (acronym "MALLAR") and, specifically, its plans for a manned spaceflight simulator and its possible application for research under contract to NASA.

During the briefing, Dolan's team members mentioned an idea for reaching the Moon. Although the Vought representatives focused their analysis on the many benefits of what they called a "modular spacecraft"—one in which different parts, including a lunar landing module, were designed for certain tasks—Brown and Michael understood what was being advertised: the essentials of the lunar-orbit rendezvous concept. "They got up there and they had the whole thing laid out," Brown remembers. "They had scooped us" with their idea of "designing a spacecraft so that you can throw away parts of it as you go along." For the next several days, Michael walked around "with his face hanging down to the floor."

Nevertheless, the chagrined Langley engineer wrote a brief paper, confident that he had spawned his idea simultaneously and independently of all others. Furthermore, the word spread around Langley that Dolan had developed the idea of using a detachable lunar-landing module for the actual landing operation after an earlier visit to Langley when engineers in the Pilotless Aircraft Research Division, who were somehow familiar with Michael's embryonic idea, had suggested a parking orbit. This explanation, however, may simply have been "sour grapes." On the other hand, Dolan had made several visits to Langley in late 1959 and early 1960, and Michael remembered having already mentioned his idea to a few people at the laboratory, "so it shouldn't have been any surprise to anybody here at Langley that such a possibility existed."[15] The truth about this will probably never be known.

What is known is that Michael's paper, at least in retrospect, had some significant limitations. It was only two pages long and presented little analysis. Its charts were difficult to follow and interpret. There was no mention of "Earth-escape weights," although an informed reader could infer such numbers by a type of inverse reasoning. Perhaps most importantly, the paper did not explicitly mention either the need for a separate lunar lander or the additional weight savings derived from using one and then discarding it before the return trip home. In sum, one would already have to have been familiar with the subject even to recognize, let alone fully fathom, what was being implied.

Michael's paper had one last problem: it was never published. Therefore, it was hardly a fully developed articulation of a lunar landing mission using lunar-orbit rendezvous. Nonetheless, Michael's unpublished paper on the weight advantages of a parking orbit made a fundamentally important contribution: for NASA researchers contemplating lunar missions, it zeroed in on the central theme of rendezvous. As his paper concluded, the chief problems in a lunar landing mission were the "complications involved in requiring a rendezvous with the components left in the parking orbit."[16]

Although disappointed that Vought had already hit on the idea of lunar-orbit rendezvous, the Langley researchers were hardly demoralized. Staffers in and around Brown's division quickly began making lunar and planetary mission feasibility studies of their own. John P. Gapcynski, for example, considered "factors involved in the departure of a vehicle from a circular orbit about the Earth." Wilbur L. Mayo calculated energy and mass requirements for missions to the Moon and even to Mars. Robert H. Tolson studied the effects on lunar trajectories of such geometrical constraints as the eccentricity of the Moon's orbit and the oblate shape of the Earth; he also analyzed the influence of the solar gravitational field. John D. Bird, who worked across the hall from Michael, began designing different "lunar bugs," "lunar schooners," and other types of small excursion modules that could land on the surface of the Moon after departing a "mother ship." "Jaybird" (as Bird was called by his peers) became an outspoken advocate of the lunar-orbit rendezvous concept. When a skeptical visitor to Langley offered, with a chuckle, that lunar-orbit rendezvous was "like putting a guy in an airplane without a parachute and having him make a midair transfer," Bird set that visitor straight. "No," he corrected, "It's like having a big ship moored in the harbor while a little rowboat leaves it, goes ashore, and comes back again."[17]

The Rendezvous Committees

There was a growing feeling within NASA in late 1959 and early 1960 that a rendezvous in space was going to be a vital maneuver no matter what the agency's mission after Project Mercury might be. If it were a space station, travel vehicles would have to meet and dock with that station and then leave it. Thus NASA had to be able to bring two vehicles together in space. A lunar mission, too, would require some sort of rendezvous either in lunar orbit, as Michael's study suggested, or around the Earth from an orbital base—perhaps the space station itself—where a lunar-bound spacecraft might be assembled or at least fueled. Even if neither were done, there would still be communications and military "reconnaissance" satellites to inspect and repair, which would also require rendezvous maneuvers. Rendezvous had to be a central element of all future flight endeavors—whatever they might be.

By the late summer of 1959, Langley's senior staff was ready to proceed with detailed studies of how best to perform rendezvous maneuvers in space. Two rendezvous study committees eventually came to life, both chaired by Dr. John C. Houbolt, the assistant chief of Langley's Dynamic Loads Division.

Houbolt (with a B.S. and M.S. in civil engineering from the University of Illinois) was an aircraft structures expert who began working at Langley in 1942. In contrast to most Langley researchers, he had some significant foreign experience, having been an exchange research scientist at the British Royal Aircraft Establishment at Farnborough, England, in 1949. In 1958, he had only recently returned from a year's education at the Swiss Federal Polytechnic Institute in Zurich, where his dissertation on the heat-related aeroelastic problems of aircraft structure in high-speed flight had earned him a Ph.D.[18]

After returning from his graduate work in Switzerland, Houbolt and many other Langley researchers in the post-Sputnik phase became increasingly curious about spaceflight. Largely independent of the conversations taking place within Brown's group, Houbolt was on his own. He said years later, "I racked down and went through the whole analysis of orbital mechanics so I could understand it." From his own preliminary studies of trajectories, he saw the vital importance of rendezvous and began to recognize and evaluate the basic problems associated with it. During the STG's training of the Mercury astronauts at Langley, Houbolt was the one who presented their course of lectures on space navigation.[19]

Houbolt especially studied one particular problem related to rendezvous in space—the timing of the launch. NASA could not launch a mission at any arbitrary time and be assured of effecting a rendezvous with an orbiting spacecraft. To visualize the problem, Houbolt built a gadget with a globe for the Earth and a small ball on the end of a short piece of coat hanger, all connected to a variable-ratio gearbox. It simulated a satellite at different altitudes and in different orbital planes, enabling him to calculate the varying amounts of time it would take for the satellite to orbit around the revolving Earth. From his considerations of orbital mechanics, he knew that a change in orbital plane at 25,000 feet per second without the help of any sort of aerodynamic lift would require an enormous amount of energy and realistically could not be made. With this simple but ingenious model, Houbolt saw how long one might have to wait—a period of perhaps many days—to launch a rendezvous mission from Cape Canaveral. But he also found a way to circumvent the problem: if the orbital plane of the satellite could be made just one or two degrees larger than the latitude of the launch site, one could extend the launch "window" to four hours every day. Thus, he began to understand how NASA could get around the long waiting periods.[20]

The word quickly spread around Langley that Houbolt, the aircraft structures specialist, was now "the rendezvous man." He even had a "license to rendezvous." The Rand Corporation, a nonprofit think-tank organization in southern California connected to Douglas Aviation and interested in space rendezvous, presented the "license" to a visiting Houbolt in early November 1959 as a jovial "pat on the back" after he had made a successful rendezvous in Douglas's rendezvous simulator.[21] Thus when NASA Langley created its steering groups to study the problems of orbital space stations and those of lunar exploration missions, Houbolt, already recognized as a brilliant analyst, naturally emerged as the one to provide the input about rendezvous.

The first of Houbolt's rendezvous committees was tied to Langley's Manned Space Laboratory Group. Headed by the Full-Scale Research Division's Mark R. Nichols, an aerodynamics specialist who was reluctant to accept the assignment, this group came to life in the late summer of 1959. It was similar to Brown's interdivisional Lunar Exploration Working Group, except that it was larger and had committees of its own. One of them, Houbolt's committee, was supposed to investigate the matter of rendezvous as it pertained to Earth-orbital operations. And it did—in a "loosely organized and largely unscheduled" way—into the first months of 1960. Serving on the committee were John M. Eggleston, Arthur W. Vogeley, Max C. Kurbjun, and W. Hewitt Phillips of the Aero-Space Mechanics Division; John A. Dodgen and William C. Mace of the Instrument Research Division; and John Bird and Clint Brown of the Theoretical Mechanics Division.[22] Given the overlapping memberships and responsibilities of the different committees and study groups created during this increasingly busy and chaotic period, it is no wonder that there has been so much confusion in the historical record about how the concept of lunar-orbit rendezvous first germinated in NASA and about who deserves credit for what.

At one of the early meetings of the Manned Space Laboratory Group on 18 September 1959, Houbolt made a long statement on the rendezvous problem, one of the first made anywhere inside the NASA family. He insisted that his committee be allowed to study rendezvous "in the broadest terms" possible because, as he presciently argued, the technique was bound to play a major role in almost any advanced space mission NASA might initiate.[23] Three months later, in December 1959, Houbolt appeared with other leading members of the Manned Space Laboratory Group before a meeting of the Goett Committee studying NASA's long-term plans. He urged the adoption of a rendezvous-satellite experiment that could "define and solve the problems more clearly"—something similar to the essence of NASA's later project, Gemini. Most members of the Goett Committee were still focusing more narrowly on a space station and a circumlunar mission; they showed little interest at that time in his experiment idea.[24]

The second Houbolt rendezvous committee met for the first time six months later, on 24 May 1960. This was one year and one day before Kennedy's "landing on the moon in this decade" speech and one week after representatives from the Goddard and Marshall Space Flight Centers and the Jet Propulsion Laboratory had met at Langley (16–17 May 1961) for an intercenter review of NASA's current rendezvous studies. At this meeting—at which Houbolt gave the principal Langley presentation (based on a paper he had just delivered at the national aeronautical meeting of the Society of Automotive Engineers in New York City, 5–8 April)—there was "complete agreement" that rendezvous was "an important problem area" that opened "many operational possibilities" and warranted "significant study." The strength of Houbolt's presentation made it obvious that of all the NASA centers, Langley was "expending the greatest effort on rendezvous." It had eleven studies under way, compared to three at the Ames Research Center and two each at the Lewis Research Center and the Flight Research Center. The Marshall Space Flight Center had an active interest in rendezvous only in connection with advanced Saturn missions. With their "leanings toward orbital operations," Wernher von Braun's people at Marshall had done little work specifically on rendezvous and were not prepared to talk about it.[25]

This second rendezvous committee was part of the Lunar Mission Steering Group created by Floyd L. Thompson, who had become Langley Research Center Director in

1960. Chairing the group was hypersonics specialist John V. Becker, chief of the Aero-Physics Division.[26] Becker's organization incorporated the Brown group, with the dynamic Brown himself serving as the chair of a committee on trajectories and guidance. Five other committees were quickly organized, with Howard B. Edwards of the Instrument Research Division chairing an instrumentation and communications committee; Richard R. Heldenfels of the Structures Research Division, a committee on structures and materials; Paul R. Hill of the Aero-Space Mechanics Division, a committee on propulsion, flight test, and dynamic loads; Eugene S. Love, Becker's assistant chief of the Aero-Physics Division, a committee on reentry aerodynamics, heating, configuration, and aeromedical studies; and John C. Houbolt, the rendezvous committee. Serving with Houbolt were John Bird and John Eggleston, who were also members of his other rendezvous committee, plus Wilford E. Sivertson, Jr., of the Instrument Research Division.

Becker's organization, as a whole, was supposed to take a "very broad look at all possible ways of accomplishing the lunar mission." At the time, NASA was conceiving it as a circumlunar rather than a landing mission. (By the late summer of 1960, Lowell E. Hasel, the secretary of Becker's study committee, was referring to the organization in his minutes as the "LaRC Circumlunar Mission Steering Group.") More specifically, the Becker group wanted to determine whether there was any reason to quarrel with the STG general guidelines for lunar missions established a month earlier, in April 1960.[27] Over the course of the next six months, this group met six times, sent representatives to NASA headquarters and the Marshall Space Flight Center for consultation and presentation of preliminary analyses, and generally educated itself in the relevant technical areas. Its exploratory experimental data eventually appeared in twelve Langley papers presented at the first Industry-NASA Apollo Technical Conference held in Washington, D.C., 18–20 July 1961. Long before, however, Langley's Lunar Mission Steering Group had discontinued its activities. In mid-November 1960, when the STG developed its formal Apollo Technical Liaison Plan, which organized specialists in each problem area from every NASA center, there was no longer any need for the group, so it simply quit meeting.[28]

Houbolt's First Crusade

In his paper presented before the Society of Automotive Engineers, of all organizations, in April 1960, 41-year-old John Cornelius Houbolt focused on "the problem of rendezvous in space, involving, for example, the ascent of a satellite or space ferry as to make a soft contact with another satellite or space station already in orbit." His analysis of "soft rendezvous" could have applied to a lunar mission, but the paper did not specifically refer to that possibility.[29]

John C. Houbolt at the time of the lunar-orbit rendezvous debate.

However, Houbolt already had been studying such an application. This was clear from the minutes of a meeting of Langley's Manned Space Laboratory Group on 5 February 1960, when Houbolt discussed the general requirements of a "soft landing device" in a lunar mission involving lunar-orbit rendezvous. This discussion took place even though that particular rendezvous committee was supposed to focus more narrowly on reaching and leaving an Earth-orbiting space station.[30]

From this point on, Houbolt began to advertise the idea of lunar-orbit rendezvous in different meetings and conversations. In the spring of 1960, he talked about landing on the Moon with Robert O. Piland and various other members of NASA's Space Task Group. During the same period, he mentioned the lunar-orbit rendezvous concept to William A. Mrazek, director of the Structures and Mechanics Division at Marshall Space Flight Center, for whom he had been helping evaluate the S–IV stage (consisting of four uprated Centaur engines) of the Saturn rocket.[31]

By the early summer months of 1960, when the Lunar Mission Steering Group first began holding meetings, Houbolt already had discovered the advantages of a lunar landing mission via lunar-orbit rendezvous. Intellectually and emotionally, he had embraced the concept as his own. Sometime during the previous months, while performing "back-of-the-envelope"-type calculations to confirm how much less rocket-boosting power NASA would require if it went to the Moon via lunar-orbit rendezvous, the Langley engineer had experienced a powerful technological enthusiasm akin to a religious experience. Three years later, in a 1963 article, he described what happened: "Almost simultaneously, it became clear that lunar orbit rendezvous offered a chain reaction simplification on all 'back effects': development, testing, manufacturing, erection, countdown, flight operations, etc." Inside his head, everything "clicked" —"all would be simplified." Everything about an American lunar landing would be made much easier. "This is fantastic," he thought to himself. "If there is any idea we have to push, it is this one!" In this moment of revealed truth arose an ardent resolve: "I vowed to dedicate myself to the task." From that moment on, until NASA's selection of the mission mode for Project Apollo in July 1962, Houbolt proved to be NASA's most dedicated, active, eloquent, stubborn, and informed crusader for what came to be known as "the LOR concept."[32]

Houbolt's first chance to "convert" others in terms of what now he considered *his* LOR concept was in September 1960, when new NASA Associate Administrator Dr. Robert C. Seamans, Jr., toured the Langley Research Center during an orientation visit. Seamans had a Ph.D. in aeronautical engineering from MIT and was a former member of a National Advisory Committee for Aeronautics (NACA) technical subcommittee on aircraft stability and control. He had assumed the NASA position on 1 September, and one of his first official duties was visiting all of the agency's field centers to learn about their programs and meet their personnel. One of the many people he encountered at Langley was an excited John Houbolt, who seized the moment to speak privately about the advantages of LOR. In essence, he said that "we ought to be thinking about using LOR in our way of going to the Moon."[33]

Bob Seamans reacted with interest. Although NASA had no mandate from political leaders to begin a lunar mission, NASA headquarters was seriously planning a lunar landing program. In October 1960, it had formed a small intercenter working group to establish a preliminary program for a lunar landing. Houbolt was Langley's representative on this committee, which was chaired by George Low. Low had been the primary lunar landing enthusiast at NASA headquarters and a strong early advocate of rendezvous methods as an alternative to the direct ascent approach, which presupposed the use of the anticipated gargantuan Nova rocket and which up to that time had almost completely dominated NASA's thinking about how to conduct a lunar-landing mission.[34] Knowing Low's preference for orbital staging techniques, Seamans was inclined to listen carefully to Houbolt's arguments for LOR.

Moreover, Seamans had previously been chief engineer for the Radio Corporation of America's (RCA) Missile and Electronics Division in Massachusetts and had been involved in an Air Force study known as Project Saint—an acronym from "satellite interceptor." This "quiet but far-reaching" classified military project involved the interception of satellites in Earth orbit. Because of this earlier work, Seamans, who was exactly the same age as Houbolt, was predisposed to listen to interesting ideas about rendezvous techniques and maneuvers. Houbolt explained to him how LOR would work even if less weight than that of the entire spacecraft was left in a parking orbit. If one just left the weight equivalent to that of the spacecraft's heatshield, NASA could realize some significant savings. Impressed with the notion of how important it was to leave weight in orbit, and equally impressed with the zeal with which Houbolt expressed that notion, Seamans invited the impassioned Langley researcher to present his ideas formally before his staff in Washington.[35]

Before that, however, Houbolt was to give two other briefings on rendezvous. The first was in November 1960, to the U.S. Air Force Scientific Advisory Board at the Pentagon. The second, on 10 December, was to leading members of the Space Task Group—Paul Purser, Robert Piland, Owen Maynard, Caldwell Johnson, James Chamberlin, and Max Faget (Chair Robert R. Gilruth was not present). During both talks, Houbolt spoke about all the possible uses of rendezvous—in terms of both lunar orbit (such as a manned lunar landing) and Earth orbit (such as assembly of orbital units, personnel transfer to and rescue retrieval from a space station, proper placement of special-purpose satellites, and inspection and interception of satellites). Houbolt tried to clarify how rendezvous would be both inherently useful and technically feasible in many space missions. In other words—and historians have missed this key point—he was advocating rendezvous in general, not just the LOR concept. If Americans were going to land on the Moon with existing rocket boosters, or even with the boosters that were planned, then the United States would have to use a combination of Earth-orbit rendezvous (EOR) and LOR.

Recalling his argument years later, Houbolt said, "We would put up a component with a first booster; we would put up another component with another booster; then we would rendezvous the two of them in Earth orbit. Then we would go to the Moon with this booster system and perform the lunar-orbit rendezvous with the remaining spacecraft. The whole reason for doing it this way (via EOR) would be because the boosters were still too small." At the same time, he was also championing LOR. He lectured from charts showing a soft lunar landing conducted with both the Saturn-class rockets then in development as well as existing launch vehicles such as Atlas or Langley's innovative little Scout rocket. He concluded by emphasizing the "great advantage" of LOR—how the Earth-boost payload in a lunar landing mission would be reduced by a factor of 2 to 2.5. "I pointed out over and over again" that if these boosters could be made bigger, then NASA "could dispense with the Earth-orbit rendezvous portion and do it solely by lunar-orbit rendezvous."[36]

Houbolt recalls that neither the Air Force Scientific Advisory Board nor the STG seemed overly interested. Nor did they seem overly hostile, however. It was this apparently passive reaction to his advocacy of LOR, which he was to experience more than a few times in the coming months, that so frustrated Houbolt and eventually helped push him to bold action. Not all of the reaction was so passive. Some of it, from intelligent and influential people inside the space program, was strong, harshly worded, and negative.

On 14 December 1960, Houbolt traveled to Washington with a group of Langley colleagues to present the staff at NASA headquarters the briefing he had promised Bob Seamans three months earlier. All of the important people were in the audience, from Administrator T. Keith Glennan, Seamans, and Wernher von Braun on down through the leadership of the STG. For fifteen minutes, Houbolt moved carefully through his charts and analysis. He concluded, as he had done in the earlier briefings, with an enthusiastic statement about the weight savings—a reduction of Earth payload by a factor of a "whopping" 2 to 2.5.

When he finished, a small man with a receding hairline and a bow tie jumped up from the audience. Houbolt knew all too well who he was: the intuitively brilliant and hot-blooded Max Faget, his long-time Langley associate and present member of the STG. "His figures lie," Faget accused, rather nastily. "He doesn't know what he's talking about."

Even in a "bull session" back at Langley, Faget's fiery accusation would have been upsetting. But "in an open meeting, in front of Houbolt's peers and supervisors," it was "a brutal thing for one Langley engineer to say to another."[37] And Faget had not bothered to say this to him four days earlier during the more private STG management briefing at Langley, when Houbolt and the others, who also were to give talks at headquarters (Clint Brown, John Bird, and Max Kurbjun), had previewed their same, exact presentations. This time, he carried his vocal objections out into the hallway, even after the meeting was over.

Houbolt tried to stay calm, but clearly he was agitated. He answered the charge simply by telling Faget that he "ought to look at the study before [making] a pronouncement like that."[38] It was an "ought to" that Houbolt would be passing on to many other LOR skeptics before it was all over.

Curiously, at the same NASA headquarters briefing, Clint Brown had made an earlier presentation, based on a study he had conducted with Ralph W. Stone, Jr., of the Theoretical Mechanics Division, showing a general operational concept of an LOR plan for a piloted lunar mission. Brown's basic idea was to develop an early launch capability by combining a number of existing rocket boosters, specifically the Atlas, Centaur, and Scout. He also illustrated the advantage of rendezvous for weight reduction over the direct lunar mission. But curiously, Brown's talk—unlike Houbolt's—did not provoke any strong negative reaction.[39] Perhaps it was because Houbolt gave a more explicit analysis of the advantages of LOR over the direct approach. Perhaps it was because Brown had given his presentation first and Faget needed to build up some steam. Or it could have been personal, with Faget simply liking Brown and disliking Houbolt.

The Feelings Against Lunar-Orbit Rendezvous

The basic premise of the LOR concept, which NASA would eventually develop for Project Apollo, was to fire an assembly of three spacecraft into Earth's orbit on top of a single powerful (three-stage) rocket, the Saturn V. This 50,000-pound-plus assembly would include: a mother ship or command module; a service module containing the fuel cells, attitude control system, and main propulsion system; and a small lunar lander or excursion module. Once in Earth's orbit, the last stage of the Saturn rocket would fire and expend itself, boosting the spacecraft—and its crew of astronauts—into its trajectory to the Moon. After braking into lunar orbit via the small rockets aboard the service module, two of the crew members would don space suits and climb into the lunar excursion module (LEM), detach it from the mother ship, and descend to the lunar surface. The third crew member would remain in the command module, maintaining a lonely but busy vigil in lunar orbit. If all went well, a top half, or "ascent stage," of the LEM would rocket back up, using the ascent engine provided, and redock with the command module. What remained of the lander would then be discarded to the vast darkness of space—or crashed onto the Moon, as was done in later Apollo missions for seismic experiments—and the astronauts would return home in their command ship.

One can summarize the LOR concept by referring to three "only" statements:

1. Only a specially designed lunar module (the LEM) would actually descend to the Moon's surface.

2. Only a portion of that LEM, the so-called "ascent stage," would return to dock with the command module in lunar orbit.

3. Only the command module, the Apollo capsule itself, with its protective heatshield, would fall back to Earth.

Knowing what we know now—that Americans would land on the Moon and return safely before the end of the 1960s, using the LOR method—it might be hard to imagine and appreciate the strength of feeling against the LOR concept in the early 1960s. In retrospect, we know that LOR enjoyed—as Brown, Michael, Dolan, and especially John Houbolt had said—several advantages over competitor methods. It required less fuel, only half the payload, and less brand-new technology; it did not need a monstrous rocket, such as the proposed Nova for a direct flight; and it called for only one launch from the Earth, whereas one of LOR's chief competitors, "Earth-orbit rendezvous," required two. Only the small, lightweight LEM, not the entire spacecraft, would have to land on the Moon; this perhaps was LOR's major advantage. Because the lander would be discarded after use and would not return to Earth, NASA could customize the LEM's design for maneuvering flight in the lunar environment and for landing softly on the Moon. In fact, NASA could tailor all the modules of the Apollo spacecraft independently—and without those tailorings compromising each other. One spacecraft unit performing three jobs would have forced some major compromises. But three units performing three jobs, without compromise, was another LOR advantage that no one at NASA could overlook.

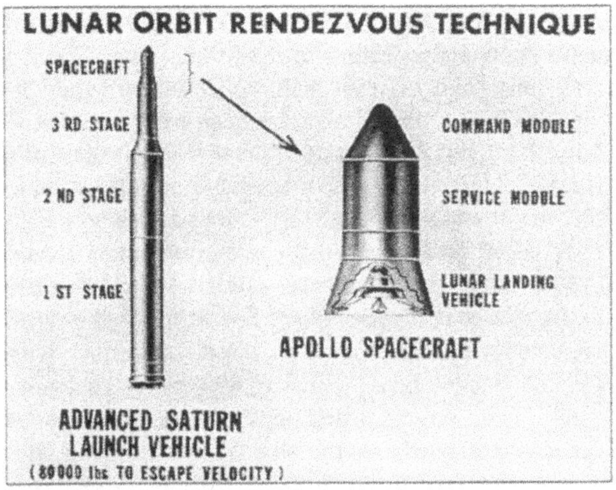

An early LOR spacecraft configuration.

In the early 1960s, however, all these advantages were merely theoretical. On the other hand, the fear that American astronauts might be left in an orbiting coffin some 240,000 miles from home was quite real. If rendezvous had to be part of the lunar mission, many felt it should be conducted only in the Earth's orbit. If that rendezvous failed, the threatened astronauts could be brought back home simply by allowing the orbit of their spacecraft to deteriorate. But if a rendezvous around the Moon failed, the astronauts would be too far away to be saved, because nothing could be done. The morbid specter of dead astronauts sailing around the Moon haunted the dreams of those responsible for the Apollo program. It was a nightmare that made objective evaluation of the LOR concept by NASA unusually difficult.

It also was a nightmare that John Houbolt understood all too well, but he recognized that all the alternative schemes had serious pitfalls and dreadful possibilities. In fact, he was certain that all the other options involved even more perils. None of them offered a rescue possibility. In contrast, LOR offered the chance of a rescue by having two small landing modules, if NASA wished, rather than just one. One lander could be reserved with the orbiting mother ship and used only if the number-one lander encountered serious trouble. Or, in the case of an accident inside the command-and-service module, even one attached LEM could serve as a type of "lifeboat." (This actually did happen during Apollo 13, when, while the spacecraft was outward bound and 200,000 miles from the Earth, an explosion in one of the oxygen tanks within the service module caused a leak in another oxygen tank. NASA had an urgent life-threatening problem that it could only solve because it had the LEM. The astronauts headed home, without landing, temporarily occupying the LEM.) Therefore, Houbolt could not accept the charge that LOR was inherently more dangerous, but neither could he easily turn that charge aside.

It was an amazingly tempestuous intellectual and emotional climate in which NASA would have to make perhaps the most fundamental decision in its history. It was a psychological obstacle that made the entire year of 1961 and the first seven months of 1962 the most hectic and challenging period of John Houbolt's life.[40]

On 5 January 1961, Houbolt again spoke about rendezvous in Washington during the first afternoon of a historic two-day meeting of the Space Exploration

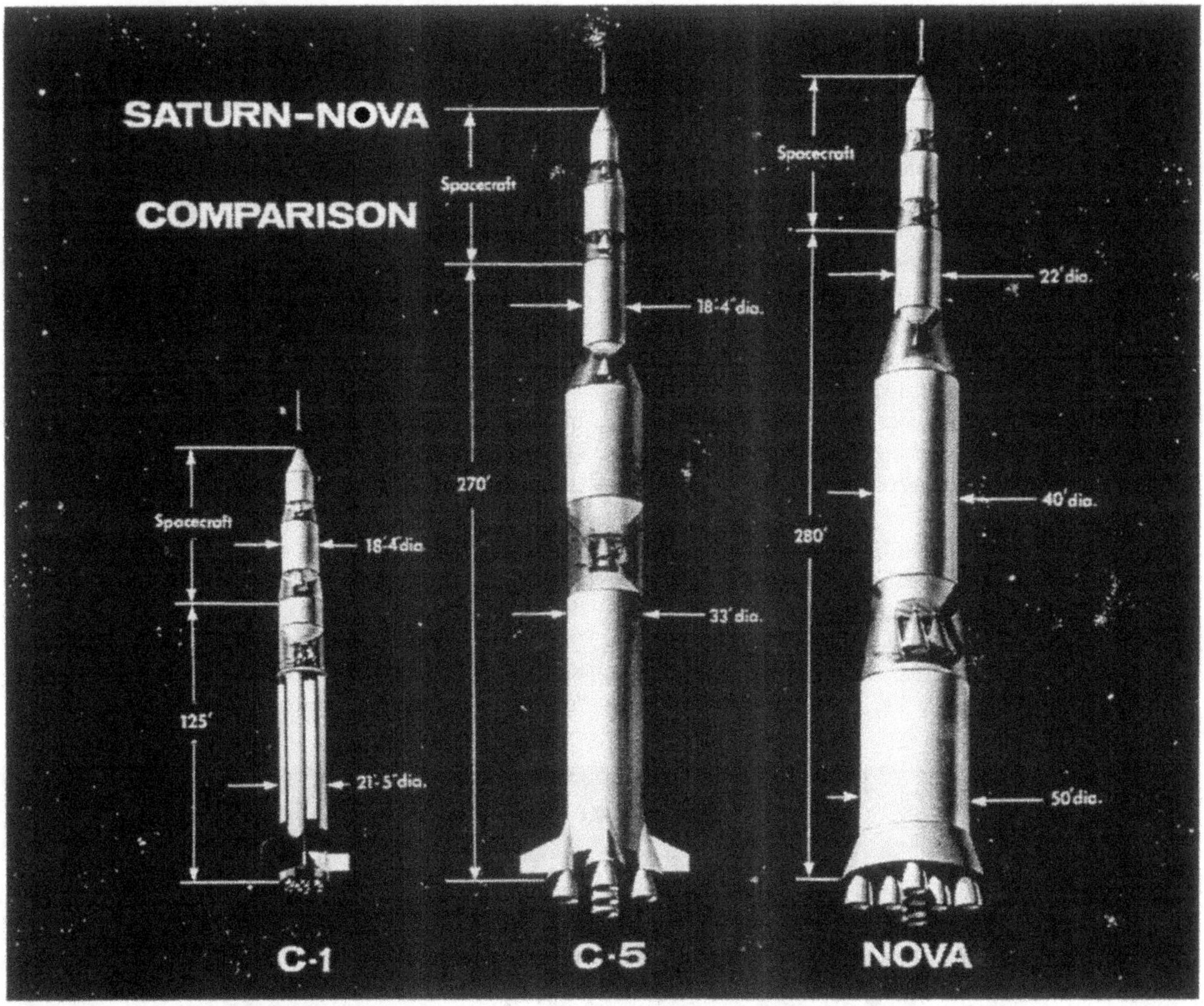

A comparison of the proposed mammoth Nova rocket with the very large Saturn C–5 and C–1 launch vehicles.
NASA #M-MS-G-36-62

Program Council at NASA headquarters. NASA had created this council for "smoothing out technical and managerial problems at the highest level." Chaired by Associate Administrator Seamans, this council meeting included, as it always did, all program office heads at headquarters, the heads of all NASA field centers, and their invited guests and speakers. The council had been meeting quarterly since early 1960, but this first meeting of 1961 was by far the most historic to date: it was the first inside NASA to feature a full-scale, agency-wide discussion of a piloted lunar landing.[41]

By the end of the first day of this meeting, everyone realized that the mission mode for a human landing on the Moon by NASA could be reduced to three major options: direct ascent, which was still the front-runner; Earth-orbit rendezvous (EOR), which was gaining ground quickly; and lunar-orbit rendezvous (LOR), the darkhorse on which only the most capricious gamblers in NASA would have ventured a bet.

A different speaker addressed each option. First, Marshall's impressive rocket pioneer from Germany, Wernher von Braun, reviewed NASA's launch vehicle program, with discussion on the advantages of Earth-orbit rendezvous. This option involved launching two pieces of hardware into space independently using advanced Saturn rockets that were then under development. The two pieces would rendezvous and dock in the Earth's orbit. The modules that had joined up during the rendezvous would allow for the assembly, fueling, and detachment of a lunar mission vehicle. That augmented ship would then proceed directly to the surface of the Moon and, after exploration, return to the Earth. The immediate advantage of Earth-orbit rendezvous, as von Braun clearly pointed out, was that it required a pair of less powerful rockets that were already nearing the end of their development—in other words, twice as many of his early Saturns. The biggest pitfall, as with direct ascent, was that there was not yet any clear concept of how the spacecraft would actually make its landing. Of that essential maneuver, von Braun offered no details, admitting that serious study would have to be conducted very quickly.

Next, Melvyn Savage of the Office of Launch Vehicle Programs at NASA headquarters talked about direct ascent. This was basically the method that had been described in science fiction novels and shown in Hollywood movies. A massive rocket, roughly the size of a battleship, would be fired directly to the Moon, land, and then blast off for home directly from the lunar surface. The trip would be like that of a chartered bus, moving from point A to point B and back to A again in one huge booster vehicle, the proposed twelve-million-pound-thrust Nova rocket.

Late in the afternoon, Houbolt discussed rendezvous and highlighted the unappreciated wonders of his darkhorse candidate. To him, the advantages of LOR and the disadvantages of the other two options were clear. Any single big rocket, such as Nova, that had to carry and lift all the fuel necessary for leaving the Earth's gravity, braking against the Moon's gravity as well as leaving it, and braking back down into the Earth's gravity again was not the most practical, especially if the mission must be accomplished soon. The development of a rocket that mammoth would take too long, and the expense would be enormous. In Houbolt's opinion, Earth-orbit rendezvous was better than direct ascent but not nearly as good as LOR. Once the lunar-bound spacecraft left its rendezvous station around the Earth, the rest of its mission would be accomplished exactly as with direct ascent. NASA's astronauts would still have to land an incredibly heavy and large vehicle on the surface of the Moon. The business of backing such a large stack of machinery down to the Moon and "eyeballing" it to a pinpoint soft landing—on what at the time was still a virtually unknown lunar surface—would be incredibly tricky and dangerous. Those few NASA researchers, such as Arthur W. Vogeley of Langley's Aero-Space Mechanics Division, who had been thinking about the terrors of landing such a behemoth (and getting the astronauts down from the top of it using an inside elevator), understood that there were no satisfactory answers to that approach.[42]

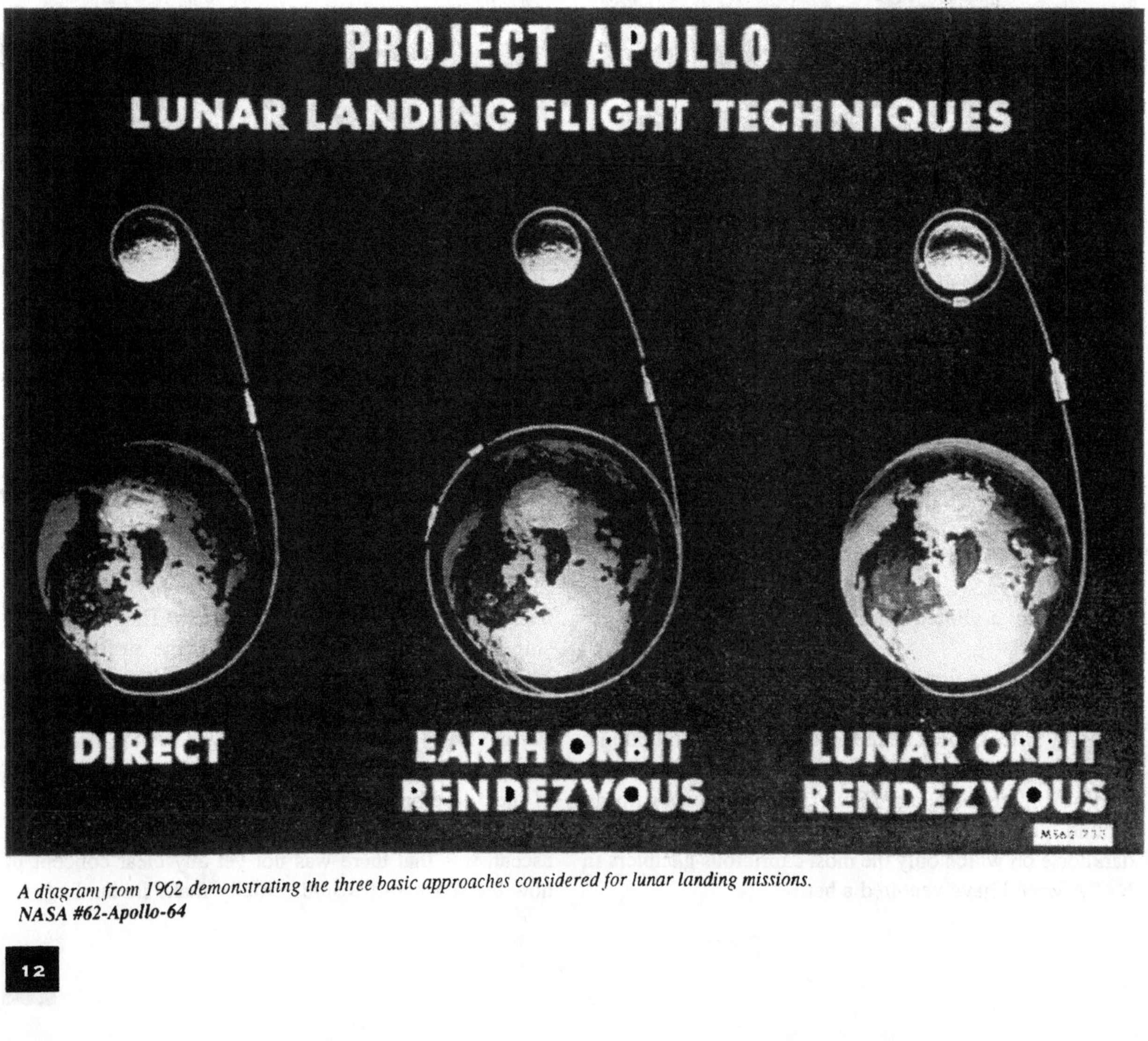

A diagram from 1962 demonstrating the three basic approaches considered for lunar landing missions.
NASA #62-Apollo-64

There were other talks that day, including an introduction by George Low, head of NASA headquarters lunar landing task force, and a technical talk by Houbolt's nemesis Max Faget that outlined the hardware and booster requirements for several possible types of lunar missions. But everyone walked away from the meeting understanding that if the United States were to reach the Moon by the end of the decade, NASA would have to evaluate the comparative benefits and risks of these three major options and somehow quickly pick the one that would work.[43] At this point, the odds were excellent that the choice—if one were to be made—would be either direct ascent, which seemed simplest in concept, or Earth-orbit rendezvous. The LOR concept was a "long shot"—almost not worthy of mention for many NASA officials.

The Space Task Group's Early Skepticism

In the early months of 1961, the STG, still at Langley, was preoccupied with the first Mercury flight and the hope—soon to be crushed by Vostok 1—that an American astronaut would be the first human in space. When any of its members had a rare moment to consider rendezvous, it was thought of "as one of several classes of missions around which a Mercury program follow-on might be built."[44]

On 10 January 1961, four days after the meeting of the Space Exploration Program Council, Houbolt and three members of the Theoretical Mechanics Division—division chief Clint Brown, Ralph Stone, and Manuel J. "Jack" Queijo—attended an informal meeting at Langley with three members of STG's Flight Systems Division—H. Kurt Strass, Owen E. Maynard, and Robert L. O'Neal. Langley Associate Director Charles Donlan, Gilruth's former chief assistant, also attended. It was at this meeting that Houbolt, Brown, and the others tried to persuade the men from the STG (Donlan had only recently been reassigned to Langley from the STG) that a rendezvous experiment belonged in the Apollo program and that LOR was preferable if any realistic plans for a lunar landing were to be made.[45]

They were not persuaded. Although the STG engineers received the analysis more politely than Max Faget had the month earlier, all four admitted quite frankly that the claims about the weight savings were "too optimistic." Owen Maynard remembers that he and his colleagues initially viewed the LOR concept as "the product of pure theorists' deliberations with little practicality." In essence, they agreed with Faget's charge, although they did not actually say it, that Houbolt's figures did "lie." In advertising the Earth-weight savings of LOR and the size reduction of the booster needed for the lunar mission, Houbolt and the others were failing to factor in, or at least greatly underestimating, the significant extra complexity, and thus added weight, of the systems and subsystems that LOR's modular spacecraft would require.[46]

This criticism was central to the early skepticism toward the LOR concept—both inside and outside the STG. Even Marshall's Wernher von Braun initially shared the sentiment: "John Houbolt argued that if you could leave part of your ship in orbit and don't soft land all of it on the moon and fly it out of the gravitational field of the moon again, you can save takeoff weight on earth." "That's pretty basic," von Braun recalled later in an oral history. "But if the price you pay for that capability means that you have to have one extra crew compartment, pressurized, and two additional guidance systems, and the electrical supply for all that gear, and you add up all this, will you still be on the plus side of your trade-off?" Until the analysis was performed (and there are some former NASA engineers who still argue today that "this trade-off has never been realistically evaluated"),[47] no one could be sure—but many NASA people suspected—that LOR would prove far too complicated. "The critics in the early debate murdered Houbolt," von Braun remembered sympathetically.[48]

Houbolt recalls this January 1961 meeting with the STG as a "friendly, scientific discussion." He, Brown, and the others did what they could to counter the argument that the weight of a modular spacecraft would prove excessive. Using an argument taken from automobile marketing, they stated that the lunar spacecraft would not necessarily have to be "plush"; an "economy" or even "budget" model might be able to do the job. One such "budget model," which the STG engineers did not seriously consider, was one of John Bird's lunar bugs, "a stripped-down, 2,500-pound version in which an astronaut descended on an open platform."[49] In answer to the charge that a complicated modular spacecraft would inevitably grow much heavier than estimated, Houbolt retaliated that the estimated weight of a direct-ascent spacecraft would no doubt increase during development, making it a less competitive option in comparison with rendezvous.

But in the end, all the substantive differences between the two groups of engineers went out the window. All Houbolt could say to the STG representatives was "you don't know what you're talking about," and all they could say to him was the same thing. "It wasn't a fight in the violent sense," reassures Houbolt. "It was just differences in scientific opinion about it."[50]

Whether or not this skeptical response to that day's arguments in favor of LOR indicated any general STG sentiment in early 1961 has been a matter of serious behind-the-scenes debate among the NASA participants. Houbolt has argued that the STG consistently opposed LOR and had to be convinced from the outside, by Houbolt himself, after repeated urgings, that it was the best mission mode for a lunar landing. Leading members of the STG, notably Gilruth and Donlan, have argued that that was not really the case. They say that the STG was too busy preparing for the Mercury flights even to bother thinking seriously about lunar studies until after Kennedy's commitment. Gilruth recalls that when Houbolt first approached him "with some ideas about rendezvousing Mercury capsules in earth orbit" as "an exercise in space technology," he did react negatively. It was a "diversion from our specified mission," according to Gilruth, and therefore not something on which he, as the head of Project Mercury, had any time to reflect.[51]

According to Gilruth, it was only later that he found out that Houbolt was interested in LOR. By that time, in early 1961, NASA had started studying the requirements of a manned lunar landing through such task forces as the Low Committee, and the STG did its best to follow suit. When it did think seriously about a lunar program, especially about that most critical operation of actually landing astronauts on the Moon, LOR gained "early acceptance . . . notwithstanding the subsequent debates that erupted in numerous headquarters committees."[52]

"I was very much in favor of that mode of flight to the moon from the very beginning," Gilruth has since claimed. "I recall telling our people that LOR seemed the most promising mode to me—far more promising than either the direct ascent or the earth orbital rendezvous modes." The most important thing in planning for a lunar landing program was to minimize the risk of the actual operation. Thus, LOR was the best choice among the contending modes because it alone permitted the use of a smaller vehicle specifically designed for the job. In Gilruth's view, he was always encouraging to Houbolt. In his estimation, he felt all along that "the Space Task Group would be the key in carrying the decision through to the highest echelons of NASA," and "of course, this proved to be the case."[53]

Houbolt accepts little of these assertions; in fact, he "violently disagrees" with them. He points out that on several occasions in late 1960 he had briefed leading members of the STG about his LOR ideas. He also asserts that Gilruth had to know about them, that the STG had ignored and resisted them as too optimistic, and that the STG would continue to ignore and resist them and insist strongly on the need for developing large Nova-class boosters for a while. As evidence, he points to many subsequent instances where his ideas were summarily discounted by the STG and to different expressions of resistance from key STG members. One such statement came from Gilruth in an official letter as late as September 1961. "Rendezvous schemes are and have been of interest to the Space Task Group and are being studied," Gilruth informed NASA headquarters on 12 September. "However, the rendezvous approach itself will, to some extent, degrade mission reliability and flight safety." Rendezvous schemes such as Houbolt's "may be used as a crutch to achieve early planned dates for launch vehicle availability," Gilruth warned. Their advocates propose them "to avoid the difficulty of developing a reliable Nova class launch vehicle."[54]

Houbolt felt strongly that if he could just persuade Gilruth's people to "do their homework" on rendezvous, "then they too would become convinced of its merits." But for months, he could not get them—or anyone else—to do that. There was "virtually universal opposition—no one would accept it—they would not even study it." In his view, it was "my perseverance, and solely mine" that caused the STG and various other groups to study and realize finally "the far-sweeping merits of the plan." It was "my own in-depth analysis" and "my crusading" based on that analysis that, above all else, later "paved the way to the acceptance of the scheme." In Houbolt's view, if not for his constant badgering, NASA might have tried to reach the Moon some other way.[55]

In early 1961, when the Low Committee announced its plan for a piloted lunar landing and its aspiration for that bold mission to be made part of Project Apollo, it definitely seemed that NASA was still resisting LOR. In outlining the requirements for an ambitious lunar flight, the committee's chief recommendation was to focus on the direct approach to the Moon, leaving rendezvous out. LOR was not discussed at all. Low remembers that during the time of his committee's deliberations, he asked one of its members, E.O. Pearson, Jr., to visit John Houbolt at Langley and "to advise the Committee whether we should give consideration to the Lunar Orbit Rendezvous Mode." Pearson, the assistant chief of the Aerodynamics and Flight Mechanics Research Division at NASA headquarters, returned with the answer, "No," LOR "was not the proper one to consider for a lunar landing." A rendezvous 240,000 miles from home, when rendezvous had never been demonstrated—Shepard's suborbital flight had not even been made yet—seemed, literally and figuratively, "like an extremely far-out thing to do." Maybe LOR would save some weight; maybe it would not. But even if it did, it

John Houbolt explaining LOR principles at a briefing in 1962.
NASA #L-62-5848

was not the best approach; too many critical maneuvers would have to be made after sending the spacecraft with its precious human cargo on its lunar trajectory. If any rendezvous had to be included, it would be much better in the Earth's orbit, where everything about the spacecraft could be thoroughly checked out and the craft brought back safely with its human occupants if something went wrong.[56]

Thus the Low Committee, in early 1961, recognizing that it would be too expensive to develop and implement more than one lunar landing mission mode, made its "chief recommendation": NASA should focus on direct ascent. "This mistaken technical judgment was not Houbolt's fault," Low admitted years later, "but rather my fault in trusting a single Committee member instead of having the entire Committee review Houbolt's studies and recommendations."[57]

Mounting Frustration

Everything that happened in early 1961 reinforced John Houbolt's belief that NASA was dismissing the LOR concept without giving it due consideration. On 20 January, he gave another long rendezvous talk at NASA headquarters. In this briefing, he displayed analysis showing a scenario for a lunar landing using Saturn rockets and outlined a simplified rendezvous scheme that had been worked out by Art Vogeley and Lindsay J. Lina of the Guidance and Control Branch of Langley's Aero-Space Mechanics Division. He also mentioned some preliminary Langley ideas for developing fixed-base simulators by which to study the requirements for lunar orbit, landing, and rendezvous.[58] Like so many of his earlier presentations, it was received passively, without much enthusiasm. On 27–28 February, NASA held an intercenter meeting on rendezvous in Washington, but no presentation on LOR was made by Houbolt or anyone else. As if by a political consensus, the subject was not even raised. This absence prompted one concerned headquarters official, Bernard Maggin from the Office of Aeronautical and Space Research, to write Houbolt a memo a few days later in which he commented on the lack of consideration for LOR by NASA, especially by the STG.[59]

Politics, of an institutional sort, were involved in the unfolding lunar landing mission mode debate. The people and organizations involved in the building of the big rockets were interested in direct ascent and even in Earth-orbit rendezvous. That type of rendezvous, although not requiring the super-big Nova booster, would still require two or more big Saturns per mission. Abe Silverstein, the director of the Office of Space Flight Programs at NASA headquarters, was working primarily from his experience as the former head of the Lewis Research Center, which was the old NACA propulsion research laboratory now heavily involved in rocket development. Wernher von Braun had to be thinking about the best interests of his Marshall Space Flight Center, which was primarily responsible at that time for developing the Saturn family of launch vehicles. What then were the politics? They centered around the concern over where the work for the overall lunar program was going to be performed. Was it to be conducted primarily by the people and organizations capable of building, managing, and launching very big rockets? By von Braun's team in Huntsville, which would need two to eight Saturn 1-class boosters to get enough weight up into Earth orbit to get to the Moon and back without having to perform LOR?[60] Or by somebody else?

For the most part, Langley management, with no such vested interest, sat on the "sidelines." No matter which mission mode was implemented, its researchers and wind tunnels would have plenty of work to support the program.[61]

In some articles and history books on Project Apollo, the LOR concept has been called a pet concept of the Langley Research Center. That was not at all the case. Even within Langley, LOR was embraced only by a small but vocal minority. Langley management did not support LOR until after the STG and the rest of NASA did. The personal opinion of Center Director Floyd Thompson, as well as that of most of his senior people, mirrored that of the STG: LOR was too complicated and risky. It was better to use direct ascent or Earth-orbit rendezvous.[62]

Houbolt was a brilliant engineering analyst—and an energetic, persistent, and often eloquent advocate of the causes he espoused—but he was not an overly shrewd behind-the-scenes player of institutional politics. Faced with the impasse of early 1961, his first instinct was simply to find more sound and logical retorts to the criticisms he had been hearing. With the help of Brown, Vogeley, Michael, Bird, Kurbjun, and a few others, he developed more elaborate and detailed studies of "his" lunar landing mission, along with detailed weight-savings analyses. Somehow, he felt, there had to be a way to circumvent the problem and convince the agency that it was making a big mistake in dismissing LOR.

On 19 April 1961, he was to give another briefing on rendezvous to the STG. Hoping to package his argument more convincingly, he turned to the use of the so-called "admiral's page." This was the established Navy practice of using a short, visually convenient executive summary so that "the admiral" would not have to "wade through the morass" of a long report. For his STG briefing, Houbolt placed sixteen pages worth of charts, data plots, drawings, and outlined analyses—taken from his own analysis as well as material supplied by Langley's Bird, Kurbjun, and Vogeley—onto one seventeen-by-twenty-two-inch foldout sheet. The title of his foldout was, "Manned Lunar Landing Via Rendezvous," and its cover included a close-up telescopic photograph of the Moon. A number of the important people attending the meeting received a copy of the printed circular and could follow along from box to box.[63]

As had been the case in Houbolt's earlier presentations, this one also addressed both Earth-orbit rendezvous and LOR, but it clearly stated a preference for LOR. In this talk, however, he advocated, for the first time, two specific projects for which he supplied project names and acronyms. He called the first ("Project 1") MORAD ("Manned Orbital Rendezvous and Docking"). This was his old idea for a modest flight "experiment" as a follow-on to Mercury that would "establish confidence" in spaceflight rendezvous techniques—a small payload from a Scout rocket serving as a target vehicle for a maneuvering Mercury capsule in the Earth's orbit. He called the second ("Project 2") MALLIR ("Manned Lunar Landing Involving Rendezvous"). It was this project, naturally, that contained the essence of the controversial LOR scheme.[64]

The last box of the foldout contained Houbolt's recommendations for "Immediate Action Required." For MORAD, he wanted NASA to give a quick "go-ahead" so that Langley could proceed with a work statement before issuing a study contract by industry. For MALLIR, he wanted NASA "to delegate responsibility to the Space Task Group" so that the STG would have to give "specific and accelerated consideration" to the possibility of including rendezvous as part of Project Apollo. In response to the STG's apparent resistance to his rendezvous ideas and its current discretionary freedom to treat rendezvous as part of Apollo on a "will also consider" basis, Houbolt wanted a NASA directive that made rendezvous integral to an accepted project. In other words, he was asking for something that would make the STG, finally, give rendezvous the attention that it merited. "I simply wanted people to study the problems and look at [them], and then make a judgment, but they wouldn't even do that," Houbolt remembers with some of his old frustration. "It was that strange a position."[65]

Nothing immediately resulted from either of his proposals. Again, the reaction seemed to him mostly negative, as if the STG still wanted no part of his ideas. His frustration mounted. "I could never find a real answer to why they wouldn't even consider it," Houbolt laments. Perhaps it was the "not-invented-here" syndrome. Perhaps it was just because he was an "outsider" who was "rocking the boat on their own thinking, and they didn't want anybody to do that."[66] Or perhaps, looking at it psychologically, the STG was not prepared to think seriously about such an incredibly bold and seemingly treacherous idea when they were not even sure they could make their own—perhaps more credible, but still difficult—Mercury program a complete success. In other words, Mercury "was proving so troublesome that rendezvous, however simple in theory, seemed very far away." Houbolt was never sure.[67]

At this April 1961 briefing, however, a solitary STG engineer did demonstrate a clear and exceptional interest in Houbolt's rendezvous analysis. James Chamberlin approached Houbolt after the meeting and asked him for an extra copy of the foldout sheet and "anything else he had on rendezvous." Interestingly, both Houbolt and Chamberlin recall Chamberlin telling him that he had known about Langley's rendezvous work but that this was the first time he had heard any of the details about the lunar orbit version.[68] One might indeed wonder then how widely the information from Houbolt's previous talks had spread within the STG. Perhaps it is significant that Chamberlin was not one of Gilruth's old associates from NACA. He was one of the relative newcomers—and a very talented one (Chamberlin had been chief of design for the Avro Arrow aircraft, an advanced airplane canceled by the Canadian government)—whom the STG had recruited from Canada in late 1959.

President Kennedy's Commitment

Houbolt's briefing to the STG came at the end of a humbling week for America. On 12 April, the Soviets beat the United States in sending the first human into space, cosmonaut Yuri Gagarin. Three days later, with President Kennedy's hesitant approval, a confused and ultimately humiliated invasion force prepared by the Central Intelligence Agency (CIA) landed at Cuba's Bay of Pigs, only to be driven back quickly by an unexpectedly efficient army of 20,000 led by communist Fidel Castro. Pierre Salinger, Kennedy's articulate press secretary, later called this "the three grimmest days" of the Kennedy presidency. It was a period of national crisis that proved in same ways to be more urgent than even the troubled aftermath of the Sputniks.[69]

Up to this time, NASA had been preparing for a lunar landing mission as its long-term goal in space. Some visionaries in NASA, such as George Low, wanted to do it sooner rather than later and were working to convince NASA leadership, now headed by a new Administrator, James E. Webb (Glennan resigned in early 1961, with the change from a Republican to a Democratic administration), that such a program should be pushed at the politicians. Not all the politicians needed to be pushed. Most notably, Vice President Lyndon B. Johnson was pressing NASA for a larger and more ambitious space program that included a lunar landing program.[70] President Kennedy was actually the one who needed to be convinced. The Gagarin flight and the Bay of Pigs fiasco, followed by the welcome relief and excitement of Alan Shepard's successful Mercury flight on 5 May, were enough to convince him. Sputniks I and II had occurred during the previous Republican administration and had helped the dynamic young senator from Massachusetts beat former Vice President Richard M. Nixon in the 1960 election. But now, in just the past month, Kennedy's "New Frontier" had been undermined by crisis. The confidence of the American people needed to be restored. Something had to provoke the country into rebounding from its recent second-place finishes in the space race and national humiliation.[71] On 25 May John Kennedy announced that landing American astronauts on the Moon was the way to restore confidence.

Houbolt's First Letter to Seamans

Six days before Kennedy's historic announcement, and oblivious that it was coming, John Houbolt sent "a hurried non-edited and limited note" of three single-spaced pages to Robert Seamans at NASA headquarters. Confident from past meetings that Associate Administrator Seamans was greatly interested in the subject of rendezvous, Houbolt took the liberty of going above several organizational layers and around his superiors to communicate with him directly.

His message was straightforward and not overly passionate. The situation with respect to the development of new launch vehicles was "deplorable"; the Saturns "should undergo major structural modifications," and there was "no committed booster plan" beyond Saturn. Furthermore, NASA was still not attending to the use of rendezvous in the planned performance of the Apollo mission. "I do not wish to argue" whether "the direct way" or "the rendezvous way" is best, Houbolt reassured Seamans. But "because of the lag in launch vehicle developments," it seemed to him that "the only way that will be available to

A high-angle view of the Saturn V launch vehicle that was used for the Apollo 15 mission to the Moon in 1971. NASA #S-71-33781

us in the next few years is the rendezvous way." For this reason alone, it was "mandatory" that "rendezvous be as much in future plans as any item, and that it be attacked vigorously."[72] If NASA continued to dismiss LOR totally as it had been, someday there were going to be sorry NASA engineers.

If Houbolt had known that an ad hoc task group at NASA headquarters was at that moment concluding that rendezvous had no place in the lunar landing program, his letter to Seamans would have carried a higher sense of urgency. But there is nothing in his letter to suggest that Houbolt knew anything about the meetings of the so-called Fleming Committee. Established by Seamans on 2 May, the job of this committee was to determine, in only four weeks, whether a lunar landing by astronauts was in fact possible and how much it would cost. Chaired by NASA's Assistant Administrator for Programs, William A. Fleming, who—unlike George Low—was known to be neutral on the ideas of a lunar landing and the method for doing it, this committee eventually recommended a lunar landing program based on a three-stage Nova. In essence, the Fleming Committee "avoided the question of rendezvous versus direct ascent." Seeing "no reason to base its study on a risky and untried alternative"—and apparently not seeing with equal clarity that going to the Moon with a huge and unproven launch vehicle was also "risky and untried"—the committee spent all its time trying to choose between solid-fuel and liquid-fuel propellants for the Nova stages.[73]

Houbolt and the other LOR advocates at Langley would have been dismayed. To them, it had been clear for some time that developing the rendezvous concept was "the obvious thing" to do before a lunar mission. But to so many others, it was still an absurdly complicated and sporty proposition.

Still others, such as Bob Seamans, were not sure what to think. On 25 May, after hearing President Kennedy's speech, Seamans appointed yet another ad hoc committee "to assess a wide variety of possible ways for executing a manned lunar landing." Whether Houbolt's letter of six days earlier played any major direct role in prompting Seamans to create this new committee, to be chaired by Bruce T. Lundin, an Associate Director at the Lewis Research Center, is not certain. But it surely contributed to it, as two pieces of circumstantial evidence seem to indicate. Houbolt still believes that Seamans created the Lundin Committee specifically because of his letter. "The story I got [from somebody else at NASA Headquarters] was that my letter jolted Seamans, and he got up at five o'clock in the morning, got on the phone, called several people and said, 'Be at my office at seven o'clock.' . . . And then they formed the Lundin Committee." There are no documents to support Houbolt's version of the story, but based on what Seamans has said about the formation of the Lundin Committee, there is no doubt that Houbolt's letter did contribute directly to its establishment—perhaps not as exclusively as Houbolt has heard. First, in explaining why a new task force was necessary, Seamans pointed out to his directors of Advanced Research Programs (Ira H. Abbott) and Launch Vehicle Programs (Don R. Ostrander) that the Fleming Committee was finding it necessary "to restrict its considerations to a limited number of techniques by which it is feasible to accomplish the mission in the shortest possible time." Consequently, there were "numerous other approaches"—and he specifically mentioned the use of rendezvous—that were not currently being assessed. Second, Seamans wrote back to Houbolt on 2 June, thanking him for his comments and reassuring the distressed Langley researcher that "the problems that concern you are of great concern to the whole agency." NASA Headquarters had just organized "some intensive study programs," Seamans informed him, without mentioning the Fleming or Lundin Committees by name. These programs "will provide us a base for decisions."[74]

It is not true, as some historians have said, that Seamans made sure that Houbolt was on the Lundin Committee.[75] Houbolt was not an official member of that committee; one of Floyd Thompson's assistants, Laurence K. Loftin, Jr., was Langley's representative, although he apparently did not attend all the meetings.

But Houbolt did meet with and talk to the committee several times; in fact, in his view, he was "the real Langley representative" because Loftin did not attend as regularly as he did.[76]

The idea behind the Lundin Committee, at least as Seamans had expressed it, was to take an open-minded look into the alternative "modes" for getting to the Moon, primarily those involving "mission staging by rendezvous" and "alternative Nova vehicles." From its initial meeting, however, that idea seems to have been seriously compromised. Larry Loftin, who attended the opening meeting in early June 1961, remembers that Seamans came in the first day and "sort of gave us our marching orders." Then Abe Silverstein, director of the Office of Space Flight Programs at NASA headquarters, came in to address the members. Silverstein said:

Well, look fellas, I want you to understand something. I've been right most of my life about things, and if you guys are going to talk about rendezvous, any kind of rendezvous, as a way of going to the Moon, forget it. I've heard all those schemes and I don't want to hear any more of them, because we're not going to the Moon using any of those schemes.

And with those words of warning and damnation, which completely violated the reason for having the committee in the first place, the usually masterful but, in this case, self-righteous Silverstein "stomped out of the room."[77]

To its credit, the Lundin Committee disregarded Silverstein's admonition and instead considered a broad range of different rendezvous schemes. With a complete analysis of the rendezvous problems by Houbolt and assorted insights from invited analysts both from inside and outside NASA, the group studied mission profiles involving rendezvous in Earth orbit, in transit to the Moon, in lunar orbit before landing, in lunar orbit after takeoff from the Moon, and in both Earth and lunar orbit. It even considered the fantastic idea of a "lunar-surface rendezvous." This involved launching a fuel cache and a few other unmanned components of a return spacecraft to the Moon's surface—a payload of about 5,000 pounds—and then landing astronauts separately in a second spacecraft whose fuel supply would be exhausted just getting there. The notion, as absurd as it now sounds, was that the landed astronauts would find the previously deposited hardware (homing beacons previously landed as part of the unmanned Surveyor program were to make pinpoint landings possible) and then assemble and fuel a new spacecraft for the return trip. Television monitoring equipment would check everything out before sending astronauts from the Earth to the landing area via the second spacecraft.

Houbolt thought this was "the most harebrained idea" he had ever heard. In the committee's final "summary rating" of the comparative value of the different rendezvous concepts, however, lunar-surface rendezvous finished only slightly lower than did his LOR. One anonymous committee member (most likely the Jet Propulsion Laboratory representative) even picked lunar-surface rendezvous as his first choice.[78]

As Houbolt remembers bitterly, the Lundin Committee "turned down LOR cold." In the final rating made by the six voting committee members (Loftin voted, Houbolt did not), LOR finished a distant third—with no first place votes, only one second, two thirds, two fourths, and one fifth or last place. Far ahead of it were two different low-Earth-orbit rendezvous schemes, the first one using two to three Saturn C–3 boosters and the other involving a Saturn C–1 plus the Nova. Both concepts were strongly favored by NASA Marshall, which by this time had embraced the idea of Earth-orbit rendezvous for its potential technological applications to the development of an orbiting space station.[79]

Houbolt was crushed when he heard the results. Having LOR placed at the same level of disdain as the ridiculous lunar-surface rendezvous was especially insulting. He had given the Lundin Committee his full-blown pitch, complete with the foldout sheet and slides. "They'd say, 'That sounds pretty good, John,' but then the next morning the same guys would come up and say, 'John, that's no good. We don't like it at all.' " For Houbolt, it was a perverse reaction to figure out. There would be an initial favorable reaction, but then "overnight, completely negative."[80] Loftin reflects back on the general fear and pessimism about LOR that ultimately ruled over the committee:

We thought it was too risky. Remember in 1961 we hadn't even orbited Glenn yet. We certainly had done no rendezvous yet. And to put this poor bastard out there, separate him in a module, let him go down to the surface and then fire him back up and expect him to rendezvous. He didn't get a second chance; it had to be dead right the first time. I mean that just seemed like a bit much.

Moreover, Loftin and the others believed—incorrectly—that there was no real way of performing a rescue mission using LOR. In Earth's orbit, if things did not go right, then NASA might still be able to save its astronauts. In his gut, Loftin felt along with the others that the idea of LOR was just "kind of absurd."[81] It was an uneasy feeling that made it difficult for the Lundin Committee to acknowledge that all the other options entailed more complicated problems.

As discouraging as everything had been for John Houbolt up to this point, things quickly got worse. On 20 June, ten days after the Lundin Committee delivered its recommendations, Bob Seamans formed yet another task force, chaired by his assistant director of Launch Vehicle Programs, Donald H. Heaton. Following up on the summary ratings and recommendations of the Lundin Committee, Seamans asked Heaton's group to focus on Earth-orbit rendezvous, establishing the program plans and the supporting resources needed to accomplish the manned lunar landing mission using rendezvous techniques.[82] Trying to stay within those guidelines, Heaton refused to let Houbolt, an official member of his committee (Langley's W. Hewitt Phillips also served on it), even talk about LOR.

Houbolt felt himself being caught in a bizarre trap of someone else's making. He was one of the strongest believers in rendezvous in the country—he was not against Earth-orbit rendezvous, he was also in favor of it. He had just returned from his well-received formal presentation on both mission modes at an international spaceflight symposium in France.[83] But he and his Langley associates had conducted the analysis, and they knew that LOR would work even better than Earth-orbit rendezvous for a lunar landing. So he pleaded with Heaton that during the committee's study of rendezvous in Earth orbit, it also should study LOR in comparison. Heaton simply answered, "We're not going to do that, John. It's not in our charter." Then Heaton challenged, "If you feel strongly enough about it, write your own lunar-orbit [minority] report."[84]

Houbolt eventually did just that. Heaton's report, which was published in late August, concluded that Earth-orbit rendezvous "offers the earliest possibility for a successful manned lunar landing."[85] In postulating the design of the spacecraft that would make that sort of lunar mission, however, the Heaton Committee previewed a baseline configuration that Houbolt regarded as a "beast." It involved "some five different pieces of hardware that were going to be assembled in the Earth-orbit rendezvous," Houbolt remembers. "It was a great big long cigar." In his opinion, such an unwieldy concept "would hurt the cause of rendezvous." NASA engineers, especially in the STG, would read the Heaton report and say, "Well, we knew it all the time; these rendezvous guys are nuts."[86]

Or they were being driven nuts. The summer of 1961 was the busiest in the lives of many NASA engineers, certainly in John Houbolt's. "I was living half the time in Washington, half the time on the road, dashing back and forth."[87] In mid-July, he was to be in Washington again, to give a talk at the Industry-NASA Apollo Technical Conference. This important meeting was to include about 300 potential Project Apollo contractors. It was so important that Langley management, in association with the STG, in the tradition of the NACA-NASA annual inspections, was holding a formal rehearsal of all its presentations prior to the conference.

Houbolt was to give his talk at the end of the day of rehearsals because he had another NASA meeting earlier that day in Washington. "I was to rush out to the airport at Washington National, get on the airplane, they were to pick me up here and then bring me to where they were having the rehearsals." However, when he arrived breathless at the airport, the airplane could not take off. In refueling the aircraft, the ground crew had spilled fuel on one of the tires, and the Federal Aviation Administration would not let the plane take off until the tire had been changed. That made Houbolt a little late—and the STG member waiting for him a little impatient. "They dashed me back to the conference room, and with all of the other rehearsals finished, "everybody was sort of twiddling their thumbs," complaining "where the hell is Houbolt?"

After a brief apology, Houbolt began his talk. Up until the end, he purposefully said nothing specifically about LOR and talked about rendezvous in general. Then he said he had three or four final slides. "There is a very interesting possibility that rendezvous offers," Houbolt ventured, similar to a lawyer who was trying to slip in some evidence that he knew the judge would not allow, "and that is how to go to the moon in a very simplified way." He then described the whole LOR concept.

People listened politely and thanked him when he had finished. "That's a damn good paper, John," offered Langley Associate Director Charles Donlan. "But throw out all that nonsense on lunar-orbit rendezvous." Houbolt remembers that Max Faget and several other members of the STG offered the same advice.[88]

This was "strike three." The Lundin Committee had been "strike one" against Houbolt—LOR was completely rejected. The Heaton Committee had been "strike two"—LOR would not even be considered. Houbolt's rehearsal talk was, in a sense, the "third strike." But at least all three had been "swinging strikes," so to speak. Houbolt had used each occasion to promote LOR, and he had given his best effort each time. Furthermore, he was to have a few more times "at bat." The "inning" was over but not the entire "ballgame."

The next "inning" in fact came quickly, in August 1961, when Houbolt met with the so-called Golovin Committee—yet another of Bob Seamans' ad hoc task forces. Established on 7 July 1961, this joint Large Launch Vehicle Planning Group—co-chaired by Nicholas E. Golovin, Seamans' special technical assistant, and Lawrence L. Kavanau of the Department of Defense—was supposed to recommend not only a booster rocket for Project Apollo but also other launch vehicle configurations that would meet the anticipated needs of NASA and the Defense Department.[89]

The committee was to concern itself only with large launch vehicle systems, so nothing necessitated an inquiry into the LOR scheme. However, three members of the NASA headquarters staff working with this group—Eldon W. Hall, Harvey Hall, and Milton W. Rosen, all of the Office of Launch Vehicle Programs—asked that the LOR concept be presented for their consideration of a mission plan.[90] This was to be done as part of a systematic comparative evaluation of three types of rendezvous operations (Earth orbit, lunar orbit, and lunar surface) and direct ascent for a piloted lunar landing. The Golovin Committee assigned the study of Earth-orbit rendezvous to the Marshall Space Flight Center, lunar-surface rendezvous to the Jet Propulsion Laboratory, and LOR to Langley. The NASA Office of Launch Vehicle Programs would provide the information on direct ascent.[91]

This commitment to a comparative evaluation of the mission modes, including LOR, constituted a critical turning point in the history of the tortuous intellectual and bureaucratic process by which NASA eventually decided on a mission mode for Project Apollo. This is not to say that the Golovin Committee would conclude in favor of LOR, because it would not. Its final, somewhat vacillating recommendation, made in mid-October after all the field centers had delivered their reports, was in favor of a hybrid rendezvous scheme that combined aspects of both Earth-orbit rendezvous and LOR. The committee's preference was clearly for some form of rendezvous. Lunar-surface rendezvous, the Jet Propulsion Laboratory's deformed baby, had been ruled out, and direct ascent was fading as a possibility. The engineering calculations were showing clearly that any single rocket that had to carry all the fuel necessary for carrying out the entire lunar mission was just not a realistic option—especially if the mission was to be accomplished anywhere close to President Kennedy's timetable. The development of a rocket that mammoth would take too long, and the expense would be enormous.

For Houbolt and the other LOR advocates, then, the work of the Golovin Committee meant the first meaningful opportunity to demonstrate the merits of LOR in a full-blown comparison with the other viable options. It was the kind of opportunity for which Houbolt had been asking in all of his previously unsuccessful briefings. When he appeared before the committee in August 1961, "they were damn impressed." They asked him, to his delight, whether the STG knew about it. Golovin turned to Aleck C. Bond, the STG's representative on the committee, and asked him to return to Langley and "check with your fellows on what they're doing about this." A few days later, Houbolt was again in front of the STG talking to them in a well-received presentation about the same thing that they had told him not to talk about just the month earlier.[92]

With the Shepard and Grissom flights accomplished and the Golovin Committee now urging them to study rendezvous, the STG members started to come around. Thus far, as other historians have noted, the STG had "seen little merit in any form of rendezvous for lunar missions" and had reserved "its greatest disdain for the lunar orbit version."[93] Now at least some of its engineers were showing solid interest. In early September 1961, Jim Chamberlin, the STG recruit from Canada who asked for Houbolt's circular and other supporting material after hearing the proposals for MORAD and MALLIR five months earlier, talked to Gilruth about an LOR plan for a lunar landing program—and for a preparatory three-flight rendezvous experiment—that sounded much like the ideas Houbolt had been pushing. This was most significant. Never before had a member of the STG seriously offered any flight plan for a lunar landing involving any sort of rendezvous in lunar orbit. Although Gilruth was not convinced of the merits of such a scheme, he was open to further evaluation.[94]

Chamberlin's notion derived in part from the STG's August 1961 proposal for an accelerated circumlunar program; this proposal appeared as an appendix to its "Preliminary Project Development Plan for an Advanced Manned Space Program Utilizing the Mark II Two-Man Spacecraft." In essence, the larger document called for the start of what became known as Project Gemini, the series of two-astronaut rendezvous and docking missions in Earth's orbit that NASA successfully carried out between March 1965 and November 1966.[95] But the seed for Project Gemini, as planted by Chamberlin at least, must also have some important connection to Houbolt's April 1961 MORAD (Manned Orbital Rendezvous and Docking) proposal.[96]

A Voice in the Wilderness

During the late summer and early fall of 1961, Houbolt was busy preparing the formal report that the Golovin Committee had requested. Except for his "admiral's page," much of the analysis in favor of LOR was still in a loose form. So along with John Bird, Art Vogeley, Max Kurbjun, and the other rendezvous people at Langley, he set out to document their research findings and demonstrate what a complete lunar landing mission using LOR would entail. The fruit of this labor was an impressive two-volume report titled, "Manned Lunar-Landing through Use of Lunar-Orbit Rendezvous." Published by NASA Langley on 31 October 1961, this report promoted what its principal author, John C. Houbolt, called a "particularly appealing scheme" for performing the president's lunar landing mission.[97]

One might have thought that this extremely thorough document would have been enough, even for a zealous crusader like Houbolt, but it was not. The Heaton Committee had submitted its final report in August 1961—a report with which Houbolt, an official member of that committee, fervently disagreed. Some "arbitrary ground rules" had kept Houbolt from talking about LOR, and, when he protested, Heaton had told him to write his own minority report. If Heaton imagined he would not do it, he was wrong.

On 15 November 1961, Houbolt fired off a nine-page letter to Seamans with two different editions of his LOR "admiral's sheet" attached to it. The Langley engineer feared that the letter might cost him his job. He was skipping proper channels, a bold move for a government employee, in appealing directly to the associate administrator, NASA's number-two official. "Somewhat as a voice in the wilderness," Houbolt's letter opened, "I would like to pass on a few thoughts that have been of deep concern to me over recent months." He then framed his concerns in terms of questions: "Do we want to go to the moon or not?, and, if so, why do we have to restrict our thinking to a certain narrow channel?" He also asked: "Why is Nova, with its ponderous size simply just accepted, and why is a much less grandiose scheme involving rendezvous ostracized or put on the defensive?" "I fully realize that contacting you in this manner is somewhat unorthodox," Houbolt admitted, "but the issues at stake are crucial enough to us all that an unusual course is warranted."[98]

Houbolt's biggest complaint was against the bureaucratic guidelines that had made it impossible for the Heaton Committee to consider the merits of LOR. "This is to me nonsense," he stated frankly. "I feel very fortunate that I do not have to confine my thinking to arbitrarily set up ground rules which only serve to constrain and preclude possible equally good or perhaps better approaches." Too often, he declared, NASA has been narrowly circumscribing its thinking:

> *[G]round rules are set up, and then the question is tacitly asked, "Now, with these ground rules what does it take, or what is necessary to do the job?" A design begins and shortly it is realized that a booster system way beyond present plans is necessary. Then a scare factor is thrown in; the proponents of the plan suddenly become afraid of the growth problems or that perhaps they haven't computed so well, and so they make the system even larger as an "insurance" that no matter what happens the booster will be large enough to meet the contingency.*

Somehow, Houbolt warned, "the fact is completely ignored that they are dealing with a ponderous development that goes far beyond the state of the art."[99]

In condemning the drive for huge and tremendously expensive new boosters and instead advertising the efficacy of a lunar mission involving LOR and more modest boosters, Houbolt did worry about the impression he might be making. He and Seamans had had "only occasional and limited contact" and really did not know each other that well. Houbolt realized that Seamans may feel that he was "dealing with a crank." "Do not be afraid of this," Houbolt pleaded. "The thoughts expressed here may not be stated in as diplomatic a fashion as they might be, or as I would normally try to do, but this is by choice." The most important thing was that Seamans heard his heartfelt ideas directly and "not after they have filtered through a score or more of other people, with the attendant risk they may not even reach you."[100]

It took two weeks for Seamans to reply to Houbolt's extraordinary letter. Seamans agreed that "it would be extremely harmful to our organization and to the country if our qualified staff were unduly limited by restrictive guidelines." He assured Houbolt that in the future NASA would be paying more attention to LOR than it had until then.[101]

Seamans also informed him that he had passed on his long letter with its attachments to D. Brainerd Holmes, who had just replaced Abe Silverstein as head of the Office of Manned Space Flight (recently renamed Space Flight Programs). Unlike Seamans, who apparently was not bothered by the letter being sent outside formal organizational channels, Holmes "didn't like it at all" and said so when he in turn passed the letter to George Low, his Director of Spacecraft and Flight Missions. Low was more forgiving. Although he conceded that it might have been better for Houbolt to have followed standard procedures, he found the basic message "relatively sound." He, too, felt that "the bug approach" may yet prove to be "the best way of getting to the moon" and that NASA needed to give it as much attention as any other alternative. At the end of the memo to Holmes in which he passed on these feelings, Low recommended that Houbolt be invited to Washington to present in detail Langley's plan for a manned lunar landing via LOR. Low also suggested that Houbolt be a member of Holmes's staff.[102]

That never happened, but another person who did join Holmes's staff at this point, Dr. Joseph F. Shea, eventually played a major role in supporting Houbolt's ideas and making the future decision in favor of LOR. A 35-year-old Ph.D. in electrical engineering, Shea arrived at NASA during the first week of January 1962 and became Holmes's deputy director for spaceflight systems. From 1956 to 1959, this energetic engineer from the Bronx had served as the systems engineer at Bell Laboratories for a radio guidance project involving the Titan I rocket. In 1959 he moved to General Motors, where he ran the advanced development operation for its A.C. Sparkplug Division. His major achievement in this job was winning a contract for developing an inertial guidance system for the Titan II.[103]

At NASA, Joe Shea found himself thrust into helping sort out the best means of accomplishing the lunar landing mission. During one of the first days in his office, Brainerd Holmes came to see him, with his copy of Houbolt's letter in hand. Shea perused the long letter and followed Holmes to Seamans's office. Seamans asked him whether he thought there was anything to Houbolt's message. After an unsure response, Seamans advised the young systems engineer that NASA really did not know how it was going to the Moon. Shea answered tactfully, "I was beginning to get the same suspicion."[104]

"Shea didn't know much about what was going on," Houbolt remembers, but quickly he became informed within days of the meeting with Seamans and Holmes about the Houbolt letter. Shea was at Langley for a private conversation with Houbolt and for a general briefing attended by Langley management and the leadership of the STG. Going into the meeting, if Shea had a preference for any one lunar mission mode, it was a weak one for Earth-orbit rendezvous. But, especially after reading Houbolt's letter to Seamans and knowing that Seamans was sympathetic to it, Shea was not against the other options. Shea was an open-minded man who "prided himself on going wherever the data took him."[105]

And the data led him toward LOR. When Houbolt finished his much-practiced pitch, the receptive Shea admitted that the analysis looked "pretty good." He then turned to Gilruth, Faget, and other members of the STG and asked them politely whether they, too, had been thinking along the lines of LOR. Having heard about the general skepticism toward Houbolt's ideas, Shea expected a negative reaction, but he did not get it. Instead, the STG leaders responded in a mildly positive way that signified to Shea, as the discussion continued, that "actually, they had been doing some more thinking about lunar-orbit rendezvous and, as a matter of fact, they were beginning to think it was a good idea."[106]

Shea returned to Washington convinced that LOR was a viable option for Apollo and that the next step for NASA was to award a contract for an even more detailed study of its potential. On 1 March 1962, eight days after astronaut John Glenn's historic three-orbit flight in Mercury spacecraft Friendship 7, NASA awarded Tom Dolan's Chance-Vought Corporation, the firm that had been one of the original proponents of the LOR concept, the contract to study spacecraft rendezvous.[107] At Langley on 29 March, a group of researchers led by Houbolt briefed a Chance-Vought team on the center's LOR research and mission plan.[108] On 2 and 3 April, Shea presented LOR as a possible mission mode for Apollo in a headquarters meeting that was attended by representatives of all the NASA centers.[109]

The final decision to select LOR for Apollo was in the making.

The LOR Decision

In the months following Houbolt's second letter to Seamans, NASA gave LOR the serious consideration for which Houbolt had been crusading. To the surprise of many inside and outside the agency, the darkhorse candidate became the front-runner. Several factors worked in its favor. First, there was growing disenchantment with the idea of direct ascent because of the time and money necessary to develop the huge Nova rocket. Second, there was increasing technical apprehension over how the relatively large spacecraft demanded by Earth-orbit rendezvous would be able to maneuver to a soft and pinpoint landing on the Moon. As Langley's expert on the dynamics of rendezvous, Art Vogeley, explained, "The business of eyeballing that thing down to the Moon really didn't have a satisfactory answer. The best thing about LOR was that it allowed us to build a separate vehicle for landing."[110]

The first major group to favor LOR was Bob Gilruth's STG. During the critical months of the Apollo mission mode debate, this group was harried not only with planning for the first Mercury orbital flight but also with packing and leaving for its new home in Houston. Once the STG's engineers started closely examining the problems of landing a spacecraft on the Moon and had the analysis confirmed by industry, they, too, saw the wisdom of the staged approach built into LOR. It possessed a certain elegance of economy that was absent in the other schemes.

During an interview in the late 1980s, Houston's Max Faget recalled the details of how the Manned Spacecraft Center finally became convinced that LOR was the right choice. By early 1962, "we found ourselves settling into a program that was not easy to run, because so many different groups were involved. In particular, we were concerned about the big landing rocket, because landing on the Moon would, of course, be the most delicate part of the mission. The landing rocket's engine, which would be controlled by the astronauts, would have to be throttleable, so that the command-and-service module could hover, and move this way and that, to find a proper place to touch down. That meant a really intimate interface, requiring numerous connections, between the two elements," as well as between Houston and the Lewis Research Center. "Accordingly, we invented a new proposal for our own and von Braun's approach. It involved a simpler descent engine, called the lunar crasher, which Lewis would do. It wouldn't be throttleable, so the interface would be simpler, and it would take the astronauts down to a thousand feet above the lunar surface. There it would be jettisoned, and it would crash onto the moon. Then there would be a smaller, throttleable landing stage for the last thousand feet, which we would do, so that we would be in charge of both sides of that particular interface."

But at that point, Faget and his colleagues in Texas "ran into a real wall." Initially, their thinking had been that the landing would be done automatically with radar and instrument control. But the astronauts, along with a growing number of NASA engineers (primarily at Langley), began to argue that the astronaut-pilots were going to need complete control during the last phases of landing and therefore required a wide range of visibility out of the descending spacecraft. How to provide that visibility "with a landing rocket big enough to get the command-and-service module down to the lunar surface and wide enough to keep it upright" was the problem that Houston began tackling in early 1962, and they found out quickly that they could not solve it. "We toyed with various concepts," Faget remembers, such as putting a front-viewing porch on the outside or a glass bubble on top of the command module similar to the cockpit of a helicopter. But all of the redesigns had serious flaws. For example, "the porch would have to be jettisoned before lift-off from the moon, because it would unbalance the spacecraft." "It was a mess," Faget admitted. "No one had a winning idea. Lunar-orbit rendezvous was the only sensible alternative."[111]

Houbolt's role in the STG's eventual "conversion" to LOR cannot be described without upsetting someone—or at least questioning the correctness of some key player's memory. Faget, Gilruth, and others associated with the Manned Spacecraft Center believe that Houbolt's activities were "useful," but hardly as vital as many others, notably Houbolt himself, believe. "John Houbolt just assumed that he had to go to the very top," Gilruth has explained, but "he never talked to me." It is Gilruth's belief that LOR "would have been chosen without Houbolt's somewhat frantic efforts." The "real work of convincing the officials in Washington and Huntsville," he says, was done "by the spacecraft group in Houston during the six or eight months following President Kennedy's decision to fly to the moon." In other words, they were the ones who sold it, first to Huntsville and then, together with von Braun, to NASA headquarters. Houbolt's out-of-channels letter to Seamans was thus irrelevant.[112]

Houbolt believes that the STG's version is self-serving "baloney." He talked to Gilruth or his people many times; they never told him that they were on his side. If Gilruth or some other influential officer in the leadership of the space program had just once said to him, "You can stop fighting. We are now on your side; and we'll take it from here," then, Houbolt says, he would have been satisfied. But they never said anything like that, and they certainly did not "during the six or eight months" after Kennedy's speech. In fact, their words always suggested the opposite. It was not until early 1962, as seen in the prodding from Joseph Shea, that the STG gave any indication that it, too, was interested in LOR.[113]

Significantly, the outsiders or third parties to the question of Houbolt's role in ultimately influencing the STG's position tend to side with Houbolt. Bob Seamans remembers nothing about the STG showing anything but disdain for LOR during 1961.[114] Nor did George Low. To the best of his recollection, "it was Houbolt's letter to Seamans that brought the Lunar Orbit Rendezvous Mode back into the picture." It was only after the letter that a group within the STG, under Owen Maynard, began to study LOR. According to Low, "the decision was finally made" about the lunar-landing mission mode "based on Houbolt's input" and on the results of the systems engineering studies carried out at the behest of Shea's Office of Manned Space Flight Systems. "Without a doubt," in Low's view, the letter Houbolt sent to Seamans in November 1961 and the discussions at headquarters that it provoked "were the start of bringing LOR into Apollo."[115]

One final piece of testimony from an informed third party supports the importance of Houbolt's role in convincing the STG of the benefits of LOR. Starting in late 1961, NACA veteran Axel Mattson served as Langley's technical liaison officer at the Manned Spacecraft Center. Mattson maintained a small office at the Houston facility for the timely transmittal of technical information between Langley and Gilruth's recently removed STG. It was not a high-profile, management-level operation at all, nor was it supposed to be. According to the agreement between Gilruth and Langley Director Floyd Thompson, Mattson was to spend most of his time with the engineers in the field who were working on the problems.[116]

In early 1962, sometime after the Shea briefing at Langley, Floyd Thompson sent Houbolt to Houston. The purpose of his visit was, in Mattson's words, "to get the STG people really to agree that [LOR] was the best way to go and to support it." Mattson brought Houbolt to almost everyone with some interest in the mission mode issue. Houbolt told them about LOR and answered all their questions. At the end of the day, Mattson felt that "it was all over. We had the support of the Manned Spacecraft Center" for LOR.[117]

Symbolically, on 6 February 1962, Houbolt and former Langley engineer Charles W. Matthews, now of the Manned Spacecraft Center, gave a joint presentation on rendezvous to the Manned Space Flight Management Council, a special body—formed by Brainerd Holmes in December 1961—to identify and resolve difficulties in the manned spaceflight program on a month-to-month basis. The two engineers compared the merits of LOR and Earth-orbit rendezvous, concluding in favor of LOR. It is worth noting that Gilruth telephoned Houbolt personally to ask him to give this talk. According to Houbolt, it was "the first concession" that Gilruth had ever made regarding LOR.[118]

As luck would have it, the call from Gilruth came on a Friday, the day before Houbolt and his family were to leave for a ski trip to Stowe, Vermont. Gilruth asked him if he could be in Washington on Monday to give the talk, and Houbolt—remembering how he had to make reservations at the resort three months in advance—reluctantly agreed. On Saturday he flew with his wife and children to Albany, New York, rented a car, and drove to the ski resort. He stayed the night, drove back to the airport in the morning, boarded an airplane, and was in Washington in time for the Monday morning meeting.

With the STG now firmly behind LOR, it boiled down to a contest between the Manned Spacecraft Center in Houston and the Marshall Space Flight Center in Huntsville. Marshall was still a bastion for those who supported Earth-orbit rendezvous. Von Braun's people recognized two things. First, Earth-orbit rendezvous would require the development of advanced versions of Marshall's own Saturn booster. Second, the selection of Earth-orbit rendezvous for the lunar landing program would require the construction of a platform in Earth orbit that could have many other uses than for Apollo, scientific and otherwise. For this reason, space station advocates—and there were many at the Alabama facility—were enthusiastic about Earth-orbit rendezvous.[119] To them, this mode of rendezvous would offer the best long-term results.

But von Braun, their own director, would disappoint them. During the spring of 1962, the transplanted German rocket designer made the altruistic decision—despite the wishes of most of his people—to support LOR. He surprised them with this shocking announcement at the end of a day-long briefing presented to Joe Shea at Marshall on 7 June 1962:

> *We at the Marshall Space Flight Center readily admit that when first exposed to the proposal of the Lunar Orbit Rendezvous Mode we were a bit skeptical—particularly of the aspect of having the astronauts execute a complicated rendezvous maneuver at a distance of 240,000 miles from the earth where any rescue possibility appeared remote. In the meantime, however, we have spent a great deal of time and effort studying the four modes [Earth-orbit rendezvous, LOR, and two Direct Ascent modes, one involving the Nova and the other a Saturn C-5], and we have come to the conclusion that this particular disadvantage is far outweighed by [its] advantages. . . .*
>
> *We understand that the Manned Spacecraft Center was also quite skeptical at first when John Houbolt advanced the proposal of the Lunar Orbit Rendezvous Mode, and*

(From left to right) Wernher von Braun meets with Robert Gilruth and other high NASA officials, George Mueller and Kurt Debus, sometime in the mid-1960s. The chart on the wall is a diagram of the Apollo 8 mission.

> *that it took them quite a while to substantiate the feasibility of the method and finally endorse it.*
>
> *Against this background it can, therefore, be concluded that the issue of "invented here" versus "not invented here" does not apply to either the Manned Spacecraft Center or the Marshall Space Flight Center; that both Centers have actually embraced a scheme suggested by a third source.... I consider it fortunate indeed for the Manned Lunar Landing Program that both Centers, after much soul searching, have come to identical conclusions.*

The persuasive von Braun then proceeded into a long elaboration on "why we do not recommend" the direct ascent and Earth-orbit rendezvous modes and "why we do recommend the Lunar-Orbit Rendezvous Mode."[120]

For Marshall employees and many other people inside NASA, von Braun's announcement seemed to represent a type of closure—that is, the culmination of a sociopolitical process that occurs in technology typically "when a consensus emerges that a problem arising during the development of a technology has been solved." In this case, it was a very undemocratic form of closure, coming from von Braun himself, with little support from his own engineers.[121] For closure to occur and LOR to become the mission mode for Apollo, it did not take any referendum or consensus; it simply took a decision made and stuck to in the face of any later opposition. Although some questions about his motives still need to be answered, one apparent factor above all seems to explain his shift in sentiment. Von Braun understood that it was absolutely necessary, if NASA were to meet President Kennedy's deadline, to proceed with the program—and no movement was possible until the decision about the mission mode was made. Both the Manned Spacecraft Center and Langley's John Houbolt had worked on von Braun to convert him to their side. In April 1962, Houbolt sent him several of the papers prepared at Langley on a lunar landing mission using LOR, including the published two-volume report. Von Braun had requested the papers personally after hearing a presentation by Houbolt at NASA Headquarters. Then von Braun sent copies of the Langley papers to Hermann Koelle, in Marshall's Future Projects Office. And after he made his unexpected announcement in favor of LOR to the stunned crowd of Marshall employees in early June, von Braun reciprocated by sending Houbolt a personal copy of his remarks. This was a noteworthy personal courtesy by von Braun to the Langley engineer. In fact, the final sentence of the cover letter asked Houbolt to "please treat this confidentially (in other words, keep it to yourself), since no final decision on the mode has yet been made."[122]

The LOR decision was finalized in the following weeks, when the two powerful groups of converts at Houston and Huntsville, along with the original band of believers at Langley, persuaded key officials at NASA headquarters, notably Administrator James Webb, who had been holding out for direct ascent, that LOR was the only way to land on the Moon by 1969. With the key players lined up behind the concept, the NASA Manned Space Flight Management Council announced that it favored LOR on 22 June 1962. On 11 July, the agency announced that it had selected that mode for Apollo. Webb made the announcement, even though President Kennedy's science adviser, Dr. Jerome Wiesner, remained firmly opposed to LOR.[123]

On the day that NASA made the public announcement, John Houbolt was presenting a paper on the dynamic response of airplanes to atmospheric turbulence at a meeting of NATO's Advisory Group for Aerospace Research and Development (AGARD) in Paris.[124] His division chief, Isadore E. ("Ed") Garrick, also was at the meeting. A talented applied mathematician who had been working at Langley since the 1930s (and who had assisted NACA's great flutter theorist Theodore Theodorsen), Garrick had witnessed the evolution of his assistant's ideas on space navigation and rendezvous. He had listened sympathetically to all of Houbolt's stories about the terrible things that had been blocking a fair hearing for LOR.

While at the AGARD meeting in Paris, Garrick noticed a little blurb in the overseas edition of the *New York Herald Tribune* about NASA's decision to proceed with LOR. Garrick showed the paper to Houbolt, who had not seen it, shook Houbolt's hand, and said, "Congratulations, John. They've adopted your scheme. I can safely say I'm shaking hands with the man who single-handedly saved the government $20 billion."[125]

In the ensuing years, whenever the question of Houbolt's importance for the LOR decision was discussed, Garrick made it clear that he was "practically certain that without John Houbolt's persistence it would have taken several more years for LOR to have been adopted." Although "the decisions of many other people were essential to the process" and although "there is no controversy that Houbolt had help from others, . . . the essential prime mover, moving 'heaven and earth' to get the concepts across, remains Houbolt himself."[126]

Conclusion

Whether NASA's choice of the LOR concept would have been made in the summer of 1962 or at any other later time without the research information, commitment, and crusading zeal of Houbolt remains a matter for historical conjecture. His basic contribution, however, and that of his associates who in their more quiet ways also developed and advocated LOR, seems now to be beyond debate. They were the first in NASA to recognize the fundamental advantages of the LOR concept, and for a critical period in the early 1960s, they also were the only ones inside the agency to foster it and fight for it. The story of the genesis of the LOR concept thus testifies to the essential importance of the single individual contribution even within the context of a large organization based on teamwork. It also underscores the occasionally vital role played by the unpopular and minority opinion. Sometimes one person alone or a small group of persons may have the best answer to a problem. And those who believe passionately in their ideas must not quit, even in the face of the strongest opposition or pressures for conformity.

Thousands of factors contributed to the ultimate success of the Apollo lunar landing missions, but no single factor was more essential than the concept of LOR. Without NASA's adoption of this stubbornly held minority opinion in 1962, the United States may still have reached the Moon, but almost certainly it would not have been accomplished by the end of the 1960s, President Kennedy's target date.

One can take this "what-if" scenario even further. Without LOR, it is possible that no one even now—near the beginning of the twenty-first century—would have landed on the Moon. No other way but LOR could solve the landing

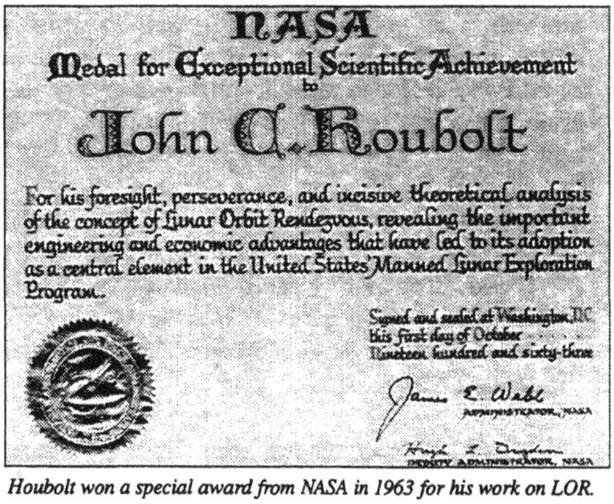
NASA
Medal for Exceptional Scientific Achievement
to
John C. Houbolt

For his foresight, perseverance, and incisive theoretical analysis of the concept of Lunar Orbit Rendezvous, revealing the important engineering and economic advantages that have led to its adoption as a central element in the United States Manned Lunar Exploration Program.

Signed and sealed at Washington, D.C. this first day of October Nineteen hundred and sixty-three

Administrator, NASA

Deputy Administrator, NASA

Houbolt won a special award from NASA in 1963 for his work on LOR.

problems. No less of an authority than George Low has expressed this same judgment. "It is my opinion to this day," Low wrote in 1982, "that had the Lunar Orbit Rendezvous Mode not been chosen, Apollo would not have succeeded." All of the other modes "would have been so complex technically, that there would have been major set-backs in the program, and it probably would have failed along the way." Low also believed that without "John Houbolt's persistence in calling this method to the attention of NASA's decision makers" and "without Houbolt's letter to Seamans (and the work that backed up that letter)," NASA "might not have chosen the Lunar Orbit Rendezvous Mode." Houbolt's commitment was a key factor in the adoption of LOR and was "a major contribution to the success of Apollo and, therefore, to the Nation."[127]

At 4:17 p.m. (eastern daylight time) on 20 July 1969, John Houbolt, by then a senior consultant with the innovative Aeronautical Research Associates of Princeton, New Jersey, sat inconspicuously as one of the "nest" of invited guests and dignitaries in the viewing room of Mission Control at the Manned Spacecraft Center in Houston. Like so many others around the world at that moment, he listened in wonder to the deliberately spoken, yet wildly dramatic words of Apollo 11 astronaut Neil Armstrong: "Houston, Tranquility Base here. The Eagle has landed."

If one ever needed some final confirmation of the importance of Houbolt's role in the selection of LOR as the mission mode for Apollo, it would come here, during the alternate cheering and shushing of that precious moment, when Americans landed and stepped on the Moon for the first time. Turning from his seat, NASA's master rocketeer, Wernher von Braun, found Houbolt's eye among all the others, gave him the okay sign, and said to him simply, "John, it worked beautifully."

Houbolt was speechless at what would be the greatest moment in his professional life—not to mention one of the greatest moments in the life of the entire human community. But the crusader was thinking: "By golly, the world ought to stop right at this moment."[128] The righteousness of his cause had been justified.

Notes

1. President John F. Kennedy, quoted in John M. Logsdon, *The Decision to Go to the Moon: Project Apollo and the National Interest* (Cambridge: MIT Press, 1970), p. 128.

2. Robert R. Gilruth, "Experts Were Stunned by Scope of Mission," *New York Times, Moon Special Supplement,* 17 July 1969. The description of Gilruth's reaction is taken from an interview, in Kilmarnock, VA, 10 July 1986, and from Charles Murray and Catherine Bly Cox, *Apollo: The Race to the Moon* (New York: Simon and Schuster, 1989), p. 16–17.

3. Robert R. Gilruth, Director of Key Personnel Development, NASA Manned Spacecraft Center, to Francis W. Kemmett, Director of the Staff, Inventions and Contributions Board, NASA headquarters, 28 August 1973. The main purposes of Gilruth's letter, which was solicited by a NASA awards board, were to evaluate Dr. John C. Houbolt's role in NASA's July 1962 decision in favor of the lunar orbit rendezvous (LOR) concept for Project Apollo and to determine whether Houbolt's contribution was worthy of the maximum prize that NASA had been authorized to give ($100,000) for an outstanding national contribution. To do that, however, Gilruth had to review the Space Task Group's position on LOR and the entire Apollo mission mode controversy. It is believed that no historian besides the author has seen this letter, which is in the author's personal LOR file. After a long investigation, the NASA Inventions and Contributions Board, chaired first by Francis Kemmett and then by Frederick J. Lees, decided not to give Houbolt the award.

4. Clinton E. Brown interview, Hampton, VA, 17 July 1989. Brown's remarks are from a panel discussion involving Brown, William H. Michael, Jr., and Arthur W. Vogeley that the author organized and led as part of Langley's celebration of the twentieth anniversary of Apollo 11, the first manned lunar landing. A videotape of the evening program featuring this panel discussion is preserved in the Langley Historical Archives (LHA), Langley Research Center, Hampton, VA.

5. William H. Michael, Jr., interview, Hampton, VA, 17 July 1989. F.R. Moulton's book on celestial mechanics was available by 1958 in a second edition (London: The MacMillan Co., 1956), but the NASA Langley library seems not to have had it. The library did get one later.

6. On the history of pioneering thoughts about and proposals for space stations, see Frederick I. Ordway III, "The History, Evolution, and Benefits of the Space Station Concept," presented to the XIII International Congress of History of Science, August 1971; Barton C. Hacker, "And Rest as on a Natural Station: From Space Station to Orbital Operations in Space-Travel Thought, 1885-1951." Both of the preceding unpublished papers are avail-

able in the archives of the NASA History Office in Washington, DC. For published information, see Wernher von Braun and Frederick I. Ordway III, *Space Travel: A History: An Update of History of Rocketry & Space Travel* (New York: Harper & Row, 1985), p. 18–20; Howard E. McCurdy, *The Space Station Decision: Incremental Politics and Technological Choice* (Baltimore and London: The Johns Hopkins University Press, 1991), p. 5–8, 237 (n. 7). On NASA's belief that a space station was the logical follow-on to Project Mercury, see Barton C. Hacker and James M. Grimwood, *On the Shoulders of Titans: A History of Project Gemini* (Washington, DC: NASA SP–4203, 1977), p. 5–6; McCurdy, *The Space Station Decision*, p. 7–9. 71.

7. Brown interview, 17 July 1989.

8. Clinton E. Brown to Eugene C. Draley, Associate Director, "Formation of a Working Group to Study the Problems of Lunar Exploration," 24 March 1959, A200–1B, Langley Central Files (LCF), Langley Research Center, Hampton, VA.

9. William H. Michael, Jr., to Eugene C. Draley, Associate Director, "Attendance at Meeting of Working Group on Lunar and Planetary Surfaces Exploration at NASA Headquarters on 14 February 1959," A200–1B, LCF; William H. Michael, Jr., "Attendance at Meeting for Discussion of Advanced Phases of Lunar Exploration at NASA Offices, Silver Spring, Md., Saturday, May 2, 1959," A200–1B, LCF. On the Jastrow Committee, see R. Cargill Hall, *Lunar Impact: A History of Project Ranger* (Washington, DC: NASA SP–4210, 1977), p. 15–16; William David Compton, *Where No Man Has Gone Before: A History of Apollo Lunar Exploration Missions* (Washington, DC: NASA SP–4214, 1989), p. 13–14.

10. Harry J. Goett to Ira S. Abbott, "Interim Report on Operation of 'Research Steering Committee on Manned Space Flight,' " 17 July 1959, A200–1B, LCF. On the Goett Committee, see Hacker and Grimwood, *On the Shoulders of Titans*, p. 9–10; Logsdon, *The Decision to Go to the Moon*, p. 56–57; Murray and Cox, *Apollo: The Race to the Moon*, p. 43–45.

11. Laurence K. Loftin, Jr., interview, Newport News, VA, 5 August 1989, copy of transcript in LHA, p. 100; Murray and Cox, *Apollo: The Race to the Moon*, p. 43–45.

12. Michael, Jr., interview, 17 July 1989.

13. W.H. Michael, Jr., "Weight Advantages of Use of Parking Orbit for Lunar Soft Landing Mission," in Lunar Trajectory Group's [Theoretical Mechanics Division] unpublished "Studies Related to Lunar and Planetary Missions," 26 May 1960, A200–1B, LCF.

14. On 13 November 1948, H.E. Ross presented the essential elements of the LOR scheme in a paper he presented before a meeting of the British Interplanetary Society in London. His conclusion was that LOR—in comparison with a direct flight to the lunar surface from the Earth—would reduce the Earth-launch weight by a factor of 2.6. In his paper Ross credited Hermann Oberth, Guido von Pirquet, Hermann Noordung, Walter Hohmann (of "Hohmann transfer" fame), Tsiolkovskiy, and F.A. Tsander for having earlier discussed ideas pertinent to the LOR concept. See H.E. Ross, "Orbital Bases," *Journal of the British Interplanetary Society* 26 (January 1949): 1–18. For a history of the first pioneering inklings about the value of rendezvous in orbit, lunar and otherwise, see Barton C. Hacker, "The Idea of Rendezvous: From Space Station to Orbital Operations in Space-Travel Thought, 1895–1951," *Technology and Culture* 15 (July 1974), as well as 1963 (supplemented 5 February 1965 and 17 February 1966), copy in the Milton Ames Collection, Box 6, LHA. The quote from Clint Brown about Michael's reaction to the Vought briefing is from Murray and Cox, *Apollo: The Race to the Moon*, p. 114–115.

15. For the Vought concept that evolved from the MALLAR study, see the Vought Astronautics brochure, *Manned, Modular, Multi-Purpose Space Vehicle*, January 1960.

16. Michael, "Weight Advantages of Use of Parking Orbit for Lunar Soft Landing Mission," p. 2.

17. The "Jaybird" story is taken from Murray and Cox, *Apollo: The Race to the Moon*, p. 115. For the technical reports that resulted from the early lunar studies in the Theoretical Mechanics Division, see, among others, J.P. Gapcynski, "A Consideration of Some of the Factors Involved in the Departure of a Vehicle from a Circular Orbit About the Earth"; W.L. Mayo, "Energy and Mass Requirements for Lunar and Martian Missions." Both articles are in the Lunar Trajectory Group's "Studies Related to Lunar and Planetary Missions." On Bird's lunar bug ideas, see Michael, Jr., interview, 7 April 1989, copy of transcript in LHA, p. 14–15. See also William H. Michael, Jr., and Robert H. Tolson, "Effect of

Eccentricity of the Lunar Orbit, Oblateness of the Earth, and Solar Gravitational Field on Lunar Trajectories," June 1960, copy in the Langley Research Center's Technical Library.

18. John C. Houbolt, "A Study of Several Aerothermoelastic Problems of Aircraft Structures in High-Speed Flight," *Eidgenoessiache Technische Hochshule Mitteilung* 5 (1956): 108 p. Throughout his career at NACA and NASA Langley, Houbolt was not a terribly prolific author of technical papers. A complete bibliography of his papers is available among the author's papers in the LHA.

19. John C. Houbolt interview, Williamsburg, VA, 24 August 1989, transcript in LHA, p. 3.

20. *Ibid.*, p. 7–8.

21. *Ibid.*, p. 9. On Rand and the early space program, see Walter A. McDougall, *Heavens and the Earth: A Political History of the Space Age* (New York: Basic Books, 1985), especially p. 89, 102, 106–110, 121–123.

22. Hacker and Grimwood, *On the Shoulders of Titans*, p. 13; Loftin, Jr., interview, 5 August 1989, p. 100–101.

23. NASA Langley, "Minutes of Meeting of LRC Manned Space Laboratory Group," 18 September 1959, A200–4, LCF. See paragraph five for Houbolt's statement on the rendezvous problem.

24. Houbolt interview, 24 August 1989, p. 9–10.

25. Bernard Maggin to Milton B. Ames, Jr., "Inter-center Discussions of Space Rendezvous," 23 May 1960; John C. Houbolt, "Considerations of the Rendezvous Problems for Space Vehicles," presented at the National Aeronautical Meeting of the Society of Automotive Engineers, New York City, 5–8 April 1960. Both documents are in A200–La, LCF. The point about Marshall's limited interest in the rendezvous problem is from Hacker and Grimwood, *On the Shoulders of Titans*, p. 14–15.

26. Lowell E. Hasel, "Minutes of Meeting of LRC Lunar Mission Steering Group," 24 May 1960, A200–1B, LCF.

27. Space Task Group, "Guidelines for Advanced Manned Space Vehicle Program," June 1960. For the summary details of these guidelines, see Ivan D. Ertel and Mary Louise Morse, *The Apollo Spacecraft: A Chronology*, Vol. I: 38–41. In brief, the STG identified a manned circumlunar mission as the "logical intermediate step" toward future goals of lunar and planetary landing. Essential to the guidelines were plans for advanced Earth-orbital missions and an Earth-orbiting space station.

28. NASA Space Task Group, "Apollo Technical Liaison Plan," 16 November 1960, A200–Lb, LCF; Langley to Space Task Group, "Langley Appointments to Apollo Technical Liaison Groups," 7 December 1960, in Project Apollo files, LCF. The following Langley researchers were appointed to the Apollo liaison groups: William H. Michael, Jr. (Theoretical Mechanics Div.), to Trajectory Analysis; Eugene S. Love (Aero-Physics Div.), to Configurations and Aerodynamics; John M. Eggleston (AeroSpace Mechanics Div.), to Guidance and Control; Robert L. Trimpi (Aero-Physics Div.), to Heating; Roger A. Anderson (Structures Research Div.), to Structures and Materials; Wilford E. Sivertson (Instrument Research Div.), to Instrumentation and Communication; David Adamson (Aero-Physics Div.), to Human Factors; and Joseph G. Thibodaux, Jr. (Applied Materials and Physics Div.), to Onboard Propulsion. Interestingly, John Houbolt was not appointed to any of the liaison groups.

On the first Industry-NASA Apollo Technical Conference, see the *Wall Street Journal*, 18 July 1961. Among the many valuable papers given by Langley's John Becker to the Archives of Aerospace Exploration at Virginia Tech, there is his file on the Lunar Mission Steering Group. On the file's cover, Becker provides a brief written introduction to the file's contents. Inside the file there is a copy of the Apollo Technical Liaison Plan, with handwritten notes by Becker. For information about this file and others in the Archives of Aerospace Exploration, contact the special collections archivist at the university library in Blacksburg, VA.

29. Houbolt, "Considerations of the Rendezvous Problems for Space Vehicles," p. 1.

30. NASA Langley, "Minutes of Meeting of LRC Manned Space Laboratory Group," 5 February 1965, A200–4, LCF. See paragraphs three and ten.

31. William A. Mrazek, Marshall Space Flight Center, to John C. Houbolt, 16 May 1960, B10–6, LCF; Houbolt interview, 24 August 1989, p. 11.

32. John C. Houbolt, "Lunar Rendezvous," *International Science and Technology* 14 (February 1963): 63. There have been several attempts to clarify the

detailed history of the genesis of LOR at Langley and Houbolt's role in it. The best efforts to date are Hacker and Grimwood, *On the Shoulders of Titans*, p. 14–16, 60–68; John M. Logsdon, "The Choice of the Lunar Orbital Rendezvous Mode," *Aerospace Historian* (June 1971): 63–70; and Murray and Cox, *Apollo: The Race to the Moon*, chaps. 8 and 9. None of them are complete, nor fully satisfy the Langley participants in the history, such as Houbolt, Michael, Brown, et al. In a footnote to their excellent book on Project Apollo, Murray and Cox remark on the holes in the overall LOR story, suggesting that "there is a fascinating doctoral dissertation yet to be written on this episode." This monograph may not close off the possibility of this doctoral dissertation, but its goal is to fill in many of the gaps and stress the Langley role in LOR.

33. Houbolt interview, 24 August 1989, p. 15; Hacker and Grimwood, *On the Shoulders of Titans*, p. 15–16.

34. Serving on the Low Committee were Eldon Hall (Office of Launch Vehicle Programs, NASA HQ), Oran Nicks and John H. Disher (both of the Office of Space Flight Programs, NASA HQ), Alfred Mayo (Office of Life Sciences Programs, NASA HQ), Earnest O. Pearson, Jr. (Aerodynamics and Flight Mechanics Research Div., NASA HQ), Heinz H. Koelle (Marshall), Max Faget (Space Task Group), and John Houbolt (Langley). See Hacker and Grimwood, *On the Shoulders of Titans*, p. 28–29. For Langley's copy of the first draft of the Low Committee report, "A Plan for a Manned Lunar Landing," 24 January 1961, see A200–1B, LCF. On the cover sheet of this report, Low identifies the members of his Lunar Landing Working Group; Houbolt's name is not included. He had been named to the committee, but he did not participate in its discussions. Nor did anyone else from Langley.

35. "RCA Will Do Saint Payload," *Aviation Week and Space Technology* 5 (December 1960): 27. For other sources on Project Saint, see Hacker and Grimwood, *On the Shoulders of Titans*, p. 416 (n. 64).

36. Houbolt interview, 24 August 1989, p. 16, 21–25. On Houbolt's final chart, there were three conclusions: (1) "Rendezvous opens possibility for earlier accomplishment of certain space measurement with existing vehicles"; (2) "There is a need for rapid development of manned rendezvous techniques—should make use of Mercury and 'Saint' technology"; and (3) "NASA should have manned rendezvous program in long-range plans with objectives of expediting soft lunar landings and flexible orbital operations."

37. Murray and Cox, *Apollo: The Race to the Moon*, p. 116.

38. Houbolt interview, 24 August 1989, p. 17–18.

39. See the reference to Brown's presentation in Charles J. Donlan to NASA Headquarters, Code KB, Director of the Staff, Inventions and Contributions, 1 March 1974. A copy of this letter is in the author's personal LOR file. John D. Bird also refers to it in "A Short History of the Development of the Lunar-Orbit-Rendezvous Plan at the Langley Research Center," 17 February 1966, p. 2.

40. The preceding two paragraphs are derived from the author's unsigned feature story, "The Rendezvous That Was Almost Missed: Lunar-Orbit Rendezvous and the Apollo Program," NASA News Release No. 89–98, 7 July 1989, p. 5–6.

41. Hacker and Grimwood, *On the Shoulders of Titans*, p. 28–29.

42. Houbolt interview, 24 August 1989, p. 21–26.

43. John I. Cumberland, Executive Secretary, Space Exploration Program Council (SEPC), to SEPC members and speakers, "Agenda for SEPC Meeting, 5–6 January 1961," A200–IB, LCF. During the first day, other technical presentations were made by Oran Nicks (Lunar and Planetary Programs, NASA HQ) on "Support by Unmanned Lunar Program"; Milton B. Ames (Office of Advanced Research Programs, NASA HQ) and E.O. Pearson (Aerodynamics and Flight Mechanics Research Div., NASA HQ) on "Research and Development Support"; and Clark T. Randt (Office of Life Sciences Programs, NASA HQ) on "Life Science Aspects."

44. Hacker and Grimwood, *On the Shoulders of Titans*, p. 29.

45. Robert L. O'Neal to Charles J. Donlan, Associate Director, "Discussion with Dr. Houbolt, LRC, Concerning the Possible Incorporation of a Lunar Orbital Rendezvous Phase as a Prelude to Manned Lunar Landing," 30 January 1961, A200–1B, LCF.

46. *Ibid.*, p. 60; Owen Maynard to Frederick J. Lees, Chairman, NASA Inventions and Contributions

Board, 13 November 1982. A copy of this letter is in the author's personal LOR file. In truth, Houbolt's numbers were overly optimistic in estimating the required weights for the lunar excursion module, because in some critical areas detailed information about the necessary subsystems was not available. Subsequent analysis by NASA and its industrial contractors provided much more realistic weight numbers. The later values for these weights did not turn out so radically out of line with Houbolt's projections; they were still within the single-launch capability of the Saturn V vehicle and therefore validated the advertised feasibility of the LOR mode for the lunar landing mission.

47. Dr. Harvey Hall to KB/Director of the Staff, NASA Inventions and Contributions Board, 28 March 1973. A copy of this letter is in the author's personal LOR file.

48. Von Braun quoted in Murray and Cox, *Apollo: The Race to the Moon*, p. 116–117.

49. *Ibid.*, p. 117.

50. Houbolt interview, 24 August 1989, p. 22.

51. Gilruth to Kemmett, 28 August 1973, p. 1; see note 2 of this monograph.

52. Donlan to Code KB, Director of the Staff, Inventions and Contributions, 1 March 1974, p. 2; see note 39 of this monograph.

53. Gilruth to Kemmett, p. 1.

54. Gilruth to Nicholas L. Golovin, 12 September 1961, quoted in Hacker and Grimwood, *On the Shoulders of Titans*, p. 61.

55. The quoted phrases are from Houbolt's letters to Francis W. Kemmett, NASA Inventions and Contributions Board, 23 May 1978 and 2 September 1981. Copies of these letters are in the author's personal LOR file.

56. The phrase "like an extremely far-out thing to do" is from George Low, quoted in Murray and Cox, *Apollo: The Race to the Moon*, p. 117.

57. George M. Low, "A Plan for Manned Lunar Landing," 24 January 1961, A220–Lb, LCF; George M. Low, President, Rensselaer Polytechnic Institute, Troy, NY, to Frederick J. Lees, NASA Inventions and Contributions Board, 21 October 1982. A copy of this letter is in the author's personal LOR file. See also E.O. Pearson, "Notes on Key Problems of Manned Lunar Missions," 13 January 1961, A200–1B, LCF.

58. See M.J. Queijo to Associate Director, "Techniques and Problems Associated with Manned Lunar Orbits and Landings," 21 February 1961, A200–1B, LCF.

59. Bernard Maggin to John Houbolt, 1 March 1961, A200–1B, LCF.

60. Brown interview, 19 July 1989. The politics also involved at least one major industrial firm, North American Aviation in Los Angeles, which already had a big contract for a command-and-service module based on the direct ascent mode. If NASA selected LOR, North American most likely would have to "share the pie" with some other contractor that would be responsible for the separate lunar lander. That contractor turned out to be Grumman. For more on the politics of the mission-mode decision, see Henry S.F. Cooper, "We Don't Have to Prove Ourselves," *The New Yorker* (2 September 1991): 64.

61. NASA Langley, "Work at LRC in Support of Project Apollo," 3 May 1961, Project Apollo file, LCF. This 15-page report divided Langley's Apollo support work into seven categories: (1) trajectory analysis, (2) configurations and aerodynamics, (3) guidance and control, (4) heating, (5) structures and materials, (6) instrumentation and communications, and (7) human factors. See also Rufus O. House to the Langley Director, "Number of Professionals in Support of Project Apollo," 19 May 1961, Project Apollo file, LCF. This memo advised center management that there were 326.5 professionals currently involved in research projects supporting Apollo, with 91 of these involved in the study of reentry heating problems.

62. Loftin interview, 5 August 1989, p. 93.

63. NASA Langley, "Manned Lunar Landing Via Rendezvous," 19 April 1961, copy in A200–1B, LCF.

64. Hacker and Grimwood, *On the Shoulders of Titans*, p. 61.

65. Houbolt interview, 24 August 1989, p. 30.

66. *Ibid.*, p. 28.

67. Hacker and Grimwood, *On the Shoulders of Titans*, p. 61.

68. *Ibid.*

69. See McDougall, *Heavens and the Earth*, p. 8, 318, 328; Murray and Cox, *Apollo: The Race to the Moon*, p. 79–80.

70. For an analysis of Lyndon Johnson's enthusiasm for the lunar mission, see McDougall, *Heavens and the Earth*, p. 319–320; Logsdon, *Decision to Go to the Moon*, p. 119–121.

71. For a more complete analysis of the political thinking behind Kennedy's lunar commitment, see chapter 15, "Destination Moon" (p. 307–324), of McDougall's *Heavens and the Earth*.

72. John C. Houbolt, Associate Chief, Dynamic Loads Division, to Dr. Robert C. Seamans, Jr., NASA Associate Administrator, 9 May 1961, copy in Box 6, Milton Ames Collection, LHA.

73. Hacker and Grimwood, *On the Shoulders of Titans*, p. 36; Murray and Cox, *Apollo: The Race to the Moon*, p. 81–82, 110. The Fleming Committee had 23 members, 18 of whom were from NASA headquarters; Langley had no representative. The members from headquarters were: Fleming, Addison M. Rothrock, Albert J. Kelley, Berg Paraghamian, Walter W. Haase, John Disher, Merle G. Waugh, Eldon Hall, Melvyn Savage, William L. Lovejoy, Norman Rafel, Alfred Nelson, Samuel Snyder, Robert D. Briskman, Secreat L. Barry, James P. Nolan, Jr., Earnest O. Pearson, and Robert Fellows. The other members were Heinz H. Koelle (Marshall), Kenneth S. Kleinknecht and Alan Kehlet (STG), A.H. Schichtenberg (The Lovelace Foundation), and William S. Shipley (Jet Propulsion Laboratory). Not surprisingly, most of these men were big-rocket specialists.

74. Robert C. Seamans, Jr., Associate Administrator, to John C. Houbolt, Associate Chief, Dynamic Loads Div., NASA Langley, 2 June 1961, copy in Box 6, Milton Ames Collection, LHA; Seamans to Director, Launch Vehicle Program (Don R. Ostrander), and Director, Advanced Research Programs (Ira H. A. Abbott), "Broad Study of Feasible Ways for Accomplishing Manned Lunar Landing Mission," 25 May 1961, A200–1B, LCF.

75. For example, Murray and Cox state that Houbolt was a member of the Lundin Committee (*Apollo: The Race to the Moon*, p. 118).

76. Loftin interview, 5 August 1989, p. 91–97; Houbolt interview, 24 August 1989, p. 32–34. Other members of the Lundin Committee, besides Lundin and Loftin, were Walter J. Downhower (Jet Propulsion Laboratory), Alfred E. Eggers (Ames), Harry O. Ruppe (Marshall), and Lt. Col. George W. S. Johnson (U.S. Air Force). Unlike the Fleming Committee, this task force—by design—had no members from NASA headquarters and was conceived to represent the technical judgments of the NASA centers.

77. Laurence K. Loftin, Jr., told this story from the audience during the 17 July 1989 videotaped celebration program for the twentieth anniversary of the Apollo 11 lunar landing. See also Loftin interview, 5 August 1989, p. 93.

78. NASA (Lundin Committee), "A Survey of Various Vehicle Systems for the Manned Lunar Landing Mission," 10 June 1961, A200–1B, LCF.

79. *Ibid.*, p. 16; Houbolt interview, 24 August 1989, p. 34.

80. Houbolt interview, 24 August 1989, p. 33; see also Murray and Cox, *Apollo: The Race to the Moon*, p. 118.

81. Loftin interview, 8 August 1989, p. 93–94.

82. Seamans to Directors for Launch Vehicle Programs and Advanced Research Programs and to Acting Director for Life Sciences Program, "Establishment of Ad Hoc Task Group or Manned Lunar Landing by Rendezvous Techniques," 20 June 1961, A200–1B, LCF. See also Hacker and Grimwood, *On the Shoulders of Titans*, p. 37–38. Serving on the Heaton Committee were ten officials from NASA headquarters, five from Marshall, one from the NASA Flight Research Center, and two from Langley. The two from Langley were Houbolt and W. Hewitt Phillips. There was also one representative from the U.S. Air Force.

83. Houbolt's paper, "Problems and Potentialities of Space Rendezvous," first presented at the International Academy of Astronautics' International Symposium on Space Flight and Reentry Trajectories, was published under the same title in *Astronautica Acta* 7 (1961): 406–429.

84. Houbolt interview, 24 August 1989, p. 39.

85. For the conclusions of the Heaton Committee, see Ad Hoc Task Group for Study of Manned Lunar Landing by Rendezvous Techniques, "Earth Orbital Rendezvous for an Early Manned Lunar Landing," Part I, "Summary Report of Ad Hoc Task Group Study," August 1961.

86. Houbolt interview, 24 August 1989, p. 39.

87. Murray and Cox, *Apollo: The Race to the Moon*, p. 119. See also Houbolt interview, 24 August 1989, p. 46.

88. Houbolt interview, 24 August 1989, p. 47–48.

89. "Report of DOD-NASA Large Launch Vehicle Planning Group, Vol. 1, 1961," copy in A200–1B, LCF. See Hacker and Grimwood, *On the Shoulders of Titans*, p. 67–68. The members of this committee, besides those mentioned in the text, were: Kurt R. Stehling and William A. Wolman (NASA HQ); Warren H. Amster and Edward J. Barlow (Aerospace Corp.); Seymour C. Himmel (Lewis); Wilson Schramm and Francis L. Williams (Marshall); Col. Matthew R. Collins (Army); Rear Adm. Levering Smith and Capt. Lewis J. Stecher, Jr. (Navy); and Col. Otto J. Glaser, Lt. Col. David L. Carter, and Heinrich J. Weigand (Air Force). There were no Langley representatives on the committee.

90. John D. Bird, "A Short History of the Development of the Lunar-Orbit-Rendezvous Plan at the Langley Research Center," final supplement, 17 February 1966, p. 3.

91. Harvey Hall, NASA Coordinator, NASA-DOD Large Launch Vehicle Planning Group, to Langley Research Center, 23 August 1961, A200–Lb, LCF.

92. Houbolt interview, 24 August 1989, p. 49.

93. Hacker and Grimwood, *On the Shoulders of Titans*, p. 60.

94. *Ibid.*, p. 55–60.

95. *On the Shoulders of Titans* is an outstanding, detailed history of the Gemini Program. For a briefer and somewhat more colorful insight into this important preparatory program for the Apollo mission, see Michael Collins, *Liftoff: The Story of America's Adventure in Space* (New York: NASA/Grove Press, 1988), p. 63–113. Better yet, see Collins' memoir, *Carrying the Fire: An Astronaut's Journeys* (New York: Macmillan, 1977). Collins, the command module pilot for the Apollo 11 mission to the Moon, was also an astronaut in the Gemini Program (Gemini-Titan X, 18–21 July 1966). His memoir is one of the best books about the manned space program of the 1960s.

96. Houbolt interview, 24 August 1989, p. 49–50.

97. NASA Langley, "Manned Lunar-Landing through Use of Lunar-Orbit Rendezvous," two vols., 31 October 1961, copy in Box 6, Milton Ames Collection, LHA. Other Langley researchers who made contributions to this two-volume report were Jack Dodgen, William Mace, Ralph W. Stone, Jack Queijo, Bill Michael, Max Kurbjun, and Ralph Briasenden. In essence, Houbolt and his associates prepared this two-volume report as a working paper that could provide, as NASA Deputy Administrator Hugh L. Dryden would later explain, "a quick summary of the information then available on LOR as a mode of accomplishing manned lunar landing and return." See Dryden to the Honorable Clinton P. Anderson, Chairman, Committee on Aeronautical and Space Sciences, U.S. Senate, 11 April 1963, copy in A200–1B, LCF.

98. John C. Houbolt, NASA Langley, to Dr. Robert C. Seamans, Associate Administrator, NASA, 15 November 1961, p. 1, copy in Milton Ames Collection, LHA.

99. *Ibid.*, p. 3.

100. *Ibid.*, p. 1.

101. Robert C. Seamans, Jr., to Dr. John C. Houbolt, NASA Langley, 4 December, 1961, copy in Box 6, Milton Ames Collection, LHA.

102. George M. Low, President, Rensselaer Polytechnic Institute, Troy, NY, to Mr. Frederick J. Less, Chairman, Inventions and Contributions Board, NASA, 21 October 1982. A copy of this letter is in the author's personal LOR file. See also Murray and Cox, *Apollo: The Race to the Moon*, p. 120.

103. For an excellent capsule portrait of Dr. Joseph F. Shea, see Murray and Cox, *Apollo: The Race to the Moon*, p. 120–125.

104. *Ibid.*, p. 124.

105. *Ibid.*

106. *Ibid.*, p. 125.

107. Ertel and Morse, *Apollo Spacecraft: A Chronology*, Vol. I: 141. On Glenn's historic flight, see Lloyd S. Swenson, James M. Grimwood, and Charles C. Alexander, *This New Ocean: A History of Project Mercury* (Washington, DC: NASA SP–4201, 1966), p. 420–436.

108. Bird, "A Short History of the Development of the Lunar-Orbit-Rendezvous Plan," p. 4.

109. NASA, "Minutes of Lunar Orbit Rendezvous Meeting, April 2–3, 1962," copy in A200–1B, LCF. See also Ertel and Morse, *Apollo Spacecraft: A Chronology*, Vol. I: 147–152.

110. Arthur W. Vogeley interview, Hampton, VA, 17 July 1989.

111. Faget quoted in Cooper, "We Don't Have to Prove Ourselves," 64. For details of the Manned Spacecraft Center's final evaluation in favor of LOR, see Charles W. Matthews, Chief, Spacecraft Research Div., MSFC, to Robert R. Gilruth, MSFC Director, "Summary of MSC Evaluation of Methods for Accomplishing the Manned Lunar Landing Mission," 2 July 1962; Robert R. Gilruth to NASA Headquarters ("Attn: Mr. D. Brainerd Holmes"), "Summary of Manned Spacecraft Center Evaluation Methods for Accomplishing the Manned Lunar Landing Mission," 5 July 1962. Both memoranda are included in Appendix A of the NASA Office of Manned Space Flight's confidential 169-page report, "Manned Lunar Landing Program Mode Comparison," 30 July 1962.

112. Gilruth to Kemmett, 28 August 1973.

113. See Murray and Cox, *Apollo: The Race to the Moon*, p. 125.

114. *Ibid.*

115. George M. Low to Frederick J. Lees, Chairman, Inventions and Contributions Board, NASA, 21 October 1982; George M. Low to John C. Houbolt, Senior Vice President and Senior Consultant, Aeronautical Research Associates of Princeton (NJ), Inc., 7 August 1969. Copies of both letters are in the author's personal LOR file.

116. For analysis of Mattson's liaison role for Langley at the Manned Spacecraft Center, see the author's book, *Spaceflight Revolution: NASA Langley Research Center from Sputnik to Apollo* (Washington: NASA SP-4308, 1995), pp. 357-369. Axel T. Mattson, Research Assistant for Manned Spacecraft Projects, to Charles J. Donlan, "Report on Activities (16–19 April 1962) Regarding Manned Spacecraft Projects," A189–5, LCF. According to Mattson's memorandum, he took Houbolt to see the following personnel of the Manned Spacecraft Center: Charles W. Matthews and John M. Eggleston (Spacecraft Research Div.), Owen Maynard and Eilsworth Phelps (Spacecraft Integration Branch), Floyd V. Bennett (Flight Dynamics Branch), and Leo T. Chauvin and William F. Rector (Apollo Spacecraft Project Office). Along with Houbolt, Langley's John D. Bird was also visiting the Houston center to discuss LOR. One of the Houston engineers with whom Houbolt and Bird met, Chuck Matthews, had just returned from a meeting at NASA Marshall. There, Matthews had reviewed Houston's thinking on the LOR concept. According to Mattson's memo, that presentation was "apparently well received by von Braun, since he made favorable comments." See also Axel T. Mattson interview, Hampton, VA, 14 August 1989, transcript in LHA.

117. Statement by Axel T. Mattson at the 17 July 1989 evening program on the twentieth anniversary of Apollo 11.

118. "Minutes of the MSF Management Council," 6 February 1962, p. 1; Houbolt interview, 24 August 1989, p. 64.

119. Brown interview, 17 July 1989; Houbolt interview, 24 August 1989, p. 68–72.

120. "Concluding Remarks by Dr. Wernher von Braun about Mode Selection for the Lunar Landing Program Given to Dr. Joseph F. Shea, Deputy Director (Systems) Office of Manned Space Flight," 7 June 1962. A copy of this 11-page document is preserved in Box 6, Milton Ames Collection, LHA. For more on von Braun's surprise announcement in favor of LOR and the reaction of the Marshall audience, see Murray and Cox, *Apollo: The Race to the Moon*, p. 139.

121. For an introduction to the concept of "closure" in science and technology, see Wiebe E. Bijker, Thomas P. Hughes, and Trevor Pinch, eds., *The Social Construction of Technological Systems: New Directions in the Sociology and History of Technology* (Cambridge and London: MIT Press, 1990), p. 12–13.

122. John C. Houbolt, Chief, Theoretical Mechanics Div., NASA Langley, to Dr. Wernher von Braun, Director, NASA Marshall, 9 April 1962, A189–7, LCF; von Braun to Houbolt, 20 June 1962. A copy of the latter is in the author's personal LOR file. Von Braun argued later that he really had not changed his mind from Earth-orbit rendezvous to LOR; he had not been a strong supporter of Earth-orbit rendezvous in

the first place. His people at Marshall had investigated Earth orbit while Gilruth's people in Houston had investigated lunar orbit, but that was part of a NASA management strategy to cover all the options thoroughly. He personally did not take sides until he had all the facts; when he did, he supported LOR. See Murray and Cox, *Apollo: The Race to the Moon,* p. 139.

123. NASA, "Lunar Orbit Rendezvous: News Conference on Apollo Plans at NASA Headquarters on July 11, 1962," copy in Box 6, Milton Ames Collection, LHA. In the press conference, Robert Seamans credited John Houbolt specifically for his contribution to the LOR concept: "I would first like to say that when I joined NASA almost two years ago one of the first places that I went to was Langley Field, and there reviewed work going on at a research base under Dr. John Houbolt. This work related both to rendezvous and what a man could do at the controls, of course under simulated conditions, as well as the possibility of lunar orbit rendezvous" (p. 8). On Wiesner's opposition to LOR, see McDougall, *Heavens and the Earth,* p. 378; Murray and Cox, *Apollo: The Race to the Moon,* p. 140–143.

Even after its July 1962 announcement in favor of LOR, NASA continued to evaluate the other major options for the Apollo mission mode. See, for example, the Office of Manned Space Flight's confidential "Manned Lunar Landing Program Mode Comparison," 30 July 1962, and the office's follow-up and also confidential "Manned Lunar Landing Mode Comparison," 24 October 1962. Copies of both documents are in A200–1B, LCF. Both reports concluded that—although some forms of Earth-orbit rendezvous were also feasible and would have adequate weight margins—on the basis of "technical simplicity, scheduling, and cost considerations," LOR was the "most suitable" and the "preferred mode."

124. John C. Houbolt, Roy Steiner, and Kermit G. Pratt, "Flight Data and Considerations of the Dynamic Response of Airplanes to Atmospheric Turbulence," July 1962.

125. Houbolt interview, 24 August 1989, p. 73.

126. I.E. Garrick, Distinguished Research Associate, NASA Langley, to Francis W. Kemmett, Code KB, NASA Inventions and Contributions Board, NASA Headquarters, 18 November 1974. Garrick wrote two other letters to Kemmett, dated 14 November 1975 and 12 September 1978. Copies of all three of these letters are in the author's personal LOR file.

127. Low to Lees, 21 October 1982, p. 2–3. On 7 August 1969, two weeks after the successful completion of the Apollo 11 mission, von Braun wrote Houbolt a personal letter in which he referred to Houbolt's "singular contribution to the Apollo program." Von Braun stated, "We know that it must be highly gratifying to you because of the rousing and complete success of your Eagle. The LM concept that you developed and defended so effectively—even, on occasion, before unsympathetic tribunals—was indeed a prime factor in the success of man's first lunar landing mission." Wernher von Braun, Director, NASA Marshall, to John C. Houbolt, Senior Vice President and Senior Consultant, Aeronautical Research Associates of Princeton (NJ) Inc., 7 August 1969, copy in the author's personal LOR file.

128. Quoted in Bill Ruehlmann, "If It Hadn't Been for Three Langley Engineers, the Eagle Wouldn't Have Landed," *The Virginian-Pilot and The Ledger-Star,* 15 July 1989. Throughout this monograph, the metaphor of Houbolt as "a crusader" is used, even though this association has plagued Houbolt for nearly thirty years. It is one of the major factors that killed his chances for getting a $100,000 cash award from the NASA Inventions and Contributions Board in the late 1970s and early 1980s (see note 3 of this monograph). This board decided, after a lengthy inquiry, that it did not give awards to individuals who simply advocated or "crusaded" for causes, however righteous they were.

One might wonder whether the NASA board did not significantly underestimate the sometimes vital role of a crusader in the ultimate success of a major technological endeavor. Most certainly in this case, the awards board used a much too literal definition of "crusader," for Houbolt was not just arguing for something for which other people were more responsible. Rather, he made LOR into a personal cause when, after extensive work on the relevant problems and his mounting frustration with NASA's failure even to consider LOR as a feasible option, he became convinced that he should crusade. "Not until I showed them all my analysis and so forth did the awards committee even realize that I had gone into so much depth in terms of working through all the various parts of the problem," says Houbolt. Or, to quote again from George Low's letter to the NASA awards committee, "it is my strongly held opinion that without the Lunar Orbit Rendezvous Mode, Apollo would not have succeeded; and that without Houbolt's letter to Seamans (and the work that backed up that letter) [author's emphasis], we might not have chosen the Lunar Orbit Rendezvous Mode" (Low to Lees, 21 October 1982, p. 3.) Despite this emphatic testimonial from one of NASA's most esteemed former officials, Houbolt received no award.

National Aeronautics and
Space Administration
Langley Research Center
Langley Field, Virginia

May 19, 1961

Dr. Robert C. Seamans, Jr.
Associate Administrator
National Aeronautics and
Space Administration
1520 H St., N.W.
Washington 25, D. C.

Dear Dr. Seamans:

This will be a hurried non-edited and limited note to pass on a few remarks about rendezvous and large launch vehicles.

First, let me comment on the staff paper on rendezvous that was recently completed by Mr. Bernard Maggin. Bernie has done a fine job here and is to be commended. I share and back the viewpoints expressed almost completely. The main item not covered is the outlining of a specific and firm program on rendezvous, but this of course could not be covered without agreement throughout NASA. We have some definite ideas on what the program should be, and these will be forwarded as soon as some reproduction problems of the material are overcome.

With respect to launch vehicles, let me forthrightedly state that the situation is deplorable:

a. To be structurally sound the Saturn should undergo major structural modifications.

b. The S-IV is having serious setbacks which make it very doubtful that any time schedule involving S-IV can be met, and further there is no back-up to this S-IV stage in case it fails completely.

c. H_2, O_2 engines are not progressing nor developing as was so gloriously promised.

d. The F-1 engine is far from being developed.

e. There is no committed booster plan beyond Saturn C-1.

f. And even the existing but payload-limited launch vehicles, such as Atlas and Titan, which have had years of development and on which tremendous funds have been spent, are operationally poor.

In brief, our booster position is pathetic, but what is even worse, we have no jobs going on or even direct plans to remedy the situation. What should be done? It would appear that any consideration should include the following:

1. Give serious deliberation as to whether S-IV should have a back-up (whether propellant is RP, storable, or solid).

2. Firm up realistic and practical boosters that go beyond Saturn C-1 capabilities.

3. Establish parallel large booster programs involving solid rockets. The potentialities of large solids have been overlooked too long, and it may very well be that they can do Saturn jobs and beyond in a relatively easy manner.

In connection with these three items, let me also make this observation which I'm sure would sound naive to many. It would come as no surprise to me that we would now have a pretty good large booster if we had concentrated effort on the development of a very simple and reliable small booster, and that all we had to do to obtain various larger boosters was to "snap" these smaller boosters together in various arrangements, with no interconnections save necessary structural coupling members.

Now, let me revert back to rendezvous. I do not wish to argue which way, the "direct way" or the "rendezvous way", is the best. But because of the lag in launch vehicle developments, it would appear that the only way that will be available to us in the next few years is the rendezvous way. For this very reason I feel it mandatory that rendezvous be as much in future plans as any item, and that it be attacked vigorously. I would like, however, to make a few comments in connection with large booster desirability. For example, the argument is presented too freely and perhaps erroneously that the cost per pound in orbit is less through use of one big booster than by other means. Not enough attention is given to reliability and to probability of mission success. If the costs based on equal probability of mission success are compared, it may very well be that the cost per pound is larger by the big booster scheme. Charts of the type shown in the attached figure should be kept in mind. In this figure the probability of a mission success is plotted against number of mission attempts, for different probabilities of success for an individual attempt. Suppose that the probability of success of a big booster attempt is 0.4, and this low value may not be unrealistic (consider the Saturn S-I engines: I understand the probability of each engine functioning is 0.96; thus, the probability of all 8 engines operating is 0.72. This value pertai to engine only; the other components may add another factor of 0.72 bringing the probability down around 0.5. Now suppose, in addition, 6 - 8 - 10 or more engines had to be ignited aloft. Surely, if it is difficult to get 8 engines going on the ground, it is even more difficult while in flight

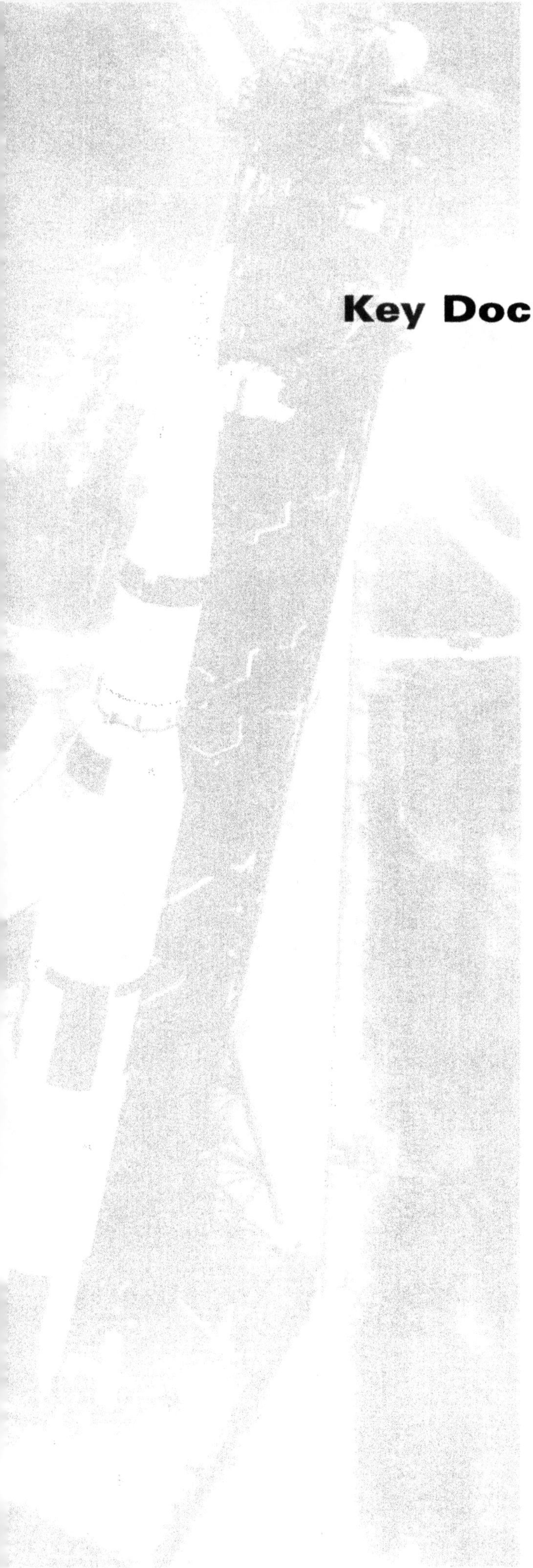

Key Documents

Thus the 0.5 may even be cut in half, giving a fairly low overall probability.) After this long side comment, let's get back to the 0.4 value. If 2 attempts at this individual probability level are involved, then the attached figure shows a 0.64 probability for mission success. In contrast, now suppose another but slightly more costly mission scheme were used which had an individual probability of 0.64. Then only one attempt is necessary to accomplish the mission with the same probability of overall success as compared with two attempts for the previous case. The net cost is thus smaller for the more costly scheme.

Additional factors which enter into big booster considerations include (1) are facilities available to construct them? (2) can they be moved about and transported? and (3) are launch sites practical and where will they be located? Although not specifically stated, one of the ideas I'm trying to bring out is that perhaps there is too much planning of projects that simply assume the existence of the type of booster needed, without asking honestly whether it really will be there, and at the right time.

I'll close now. Perhaps these thoughts may be of some use to you.

Sincerely yours,

John C. Houbolt
Associate Chief
Dynamic Loads Division

Encl.

JCH.fbm

NATIONAL
AERONAUTICS
AND SPACE
ADMINISTRATION

'61 JUN 5 AM 10:41

OFFICE OF THE ADMINISTRATOR
1520 H STREET NORTHWEST
WASHINGTON 25, D.C.
TELEPHONE: EXECUTIVE 3-3260 TWX: WA 735

IN REPLY REFER TO

June 2, 1961

Mr. John C. Houbolt
Associate Chief
Dynamic Loads Division
Langley Research Center
National Aeronautics and
Space Administration
Langley Field, Virginia

Dear John:

Thank you for your comments in your letter of May 19, 1961. As you probably know, the problems that concern you are of concern to the whole agency and we have some intensive study programs under way at the present time that will provide us a base for decisions.

You also probably know by this time that the recent Presidential recommendations for increases in the space program budget included funding for the Air Force to accelerate a large solid motor development program and an increase in the NASA budget to accelerate the rendezvous docking program.

Sincerely,

B. L

Robert C. Seamans, Jr.
Associate Administrator

National Aeronautics and
Space Administration
Langley Research Center
Langley Air Force Base, Va.

November 15, 1961

Dr. Robert C. Seamans, Jr.
Associate Administrator
National Aeronautics and
Space Administration
1520 H Street, N.W.
Washington 25, D. C.

Dear Dr. Seamans:

Somewhat as a voice in the wilderness, I would like to pass on a few thoughts on matters that have been of deep concern to me over recent months. This concern may be phrased in terms of two questions: (1) If you were told that we can put men on the moon with safe return with a single C-3, its equivalent or something less, would you judge this statement with the critical skepticism that others have? (2) Is the establishment of a sound booster program really so difficult?

I would like to comment on both these questions, and more, would like to forward as attachments condensed versions of plans which embody ideas and suggestions which I believe are so fundamentally sound and important that we cannot afford to overlook them. You will recall I wrote to you on a previous occasion. I fully realize that contacting you in this manner is somewhat unorthodox; but the issues at stake are crucial enough to us all that an unusual course is warranted.

Since we have had only occasional and limited contact, and because you therefore probably do not know me very well, it is conceivable that after reading this you may feel that you are dealing with a crank. Do not be afraid of this. The thoughts expressed here may not be stated in as diplomatic a fashion as they might be, or as I would normally try to do, but this is by choice and at the moment is not important. The important point is that you hear the ideas directly, not after they have filtered through a score or more of other people, with the attendant risk that they may not even reach you.

Manned Lunar Landing Through Use of Lunar Orbit Rendezvous

The plan.- The first attachment outlines in brief the plan by which we may accomplish a manned lunar landing through use of a lunar rendezvous, and shows a number of schemes for doing this by means of a single C-3, its equivalent, or even something less. The basic ideas of the plan were presented before various NASA people well over a year ago, and were since repeated at numerous interlaboratory meetings. A lunar landing program utilizing rendezvous concepts was even suggested back in April. Essentially, it had three basic points: (1) the establishment of an early rendezvous program involving Mercury, (2) the specific inclusion of rendezvous in Apollo developments, and (3) the accomplishment of lunar landing through use of C-2's. It was indicated then that two C-2's could do the job, C-2 being referred to simply because NASA booster plans did not go beyond the C-2 at that time; it was mentioned, however, that with a C-3 the number of boosters required would be cut in half, specifically only one.

Regrettably, there was little interest shown in the idea - indeed, if any, it was negative.

Also (for the record), the scheme was presented before the Lundin Committee. It received only bare mention in the final report and was not discussed further (see comments below in section entitled "Grandiose Plans").

It was presented before the Heaton Committee, accepted as a good idea, then dropped, mainly on the irrelevant basis that it did not conform to the ground rules. I even argued against presenting the main plan considered by the Heaton Committee, largely because it would only bring harm to the rendezvous cause, and further argued that if the committee did not want to consider lunar rendezvous, at least they should make a strong recommendation that it looks promising enough that it deserves a separate treatment by itself - but to no avail. In fact, it was mentioned that if I felt sufficiently strong about the matter, I should make a minority report. This is essentially what I am doing.

We have given the plan to the presently meeting Golovin Committee on several occasions.

In a rehearsal of a talk on rendezvous for the recent Apollo Conference, I gave a brief reference to the plan, indicating the benefit derivable therefrom, knowing full well that the reviewing committee would ask me to withdraw any reference to this idea. As expected, this was the only item I was asked to delete.

The plan has been presented to the Space Task Group personnel several times, dating back to more than a year ago. The interest expressed has been completely negative.

Ground rules.- The greatest objection that has been raised about our lunar rendezvous plan is that it does not conform to the "ground rules". This to me is nonsense; the important question is, "Do we want to get to the moon or not?", and, if so, why do we have to restrict our thinking along a certain narrow channel. I feel very fortunate that I do not have to confine my thinking to arbitrarily set up ground rules which only serve to constrain and preclude possible equally good or perhaps better approaches. Too often thinking goes along the following vein: gound rules are set up, and then the question is tacitly asked, "Now, with these ground rules what does it take, or what is necessary to do the job?". A design begins and shortly it is realized that a booster system way beyond present plans is necessary. Then a scare factor is thrown in; the proponents of the plan suddenly become afraid of the growth problem or that perhaps they haven't computed so well, and so they make the system even larger as an "insurance" that no matter what happens the booster will be large enough to meet the contingency. Somehow, the fact is completely ignored that they are now dealing with a ponderous development that goes far beyond the state-of-the-art.

Why is there not more thinking along the following lines: Thus, with this given booster, or this one, is there anything we can do to do the job? In other words, why can't we also think along the lines of deriving a plan to fit a booster, rather than derive a booster to fit a plan?

Three ground rules in particular are worthy of mention: three men, direct landing, and storable return. These are very restrictive requirements. If two men can do the job, and if the use of only two men allows the job to be done, then why not do it this way? If relaxing the direct requirements allows the job to be done with a C-3, then why not relax it? Further, when a hard objective look is taken at the use of storables, then it is soon realized that perhaps they aren't so desirable or advantageous after all in comparison with some other fuels.

Grandiose plans, one-sided objections, and bias.- For some inexplicable reason, everyone seems to want to avoid simple schemes. The majority always seems to be thinking in terms of grandiose plans, giving all sort of arguments for long-range plans, etc. Why is there not more thinking in the direction of developing the simplest scheme possible? Figuratively, why not go by a Chevrolet instead of a Cadillac? Surely a Chevrolet gets one from one place to another just as well as a Cadillac, and in many respects with marked advantages.

I have been appalled at the thinking of individuals and committees on these matters. For example, comments of the following type have been made: "Houbolt has a scheme that has a 50 percent chance of getting a man to the moon, and a 1 percent chance of getting him back." This comment was made by a Headquarters individual at 'high level who never really has taken the time to hear about the scheme, never has had the scheme explained to him fully, or possible even correctly, and yet he feels free to pass judgment on the work. I am bothered by stupidity of this type being displayed by individuals who are in a position to make decisions which affect not only the NASA, but the fate of the nation as well. I have even grown to be concerned about the merits of all the committees that have been considering the problem. Because of bias, the intent of the committee is destroyed even before it starts and, further, the outcome is usually obvious from the beginning. We knew what the Fleming Committee results would be before it started. After one day it was clear what decisions the Lundin Committee would reach. After a couple days it was obvious what the main decision of the Heaton Committee would be. In connection with the Lundin Committee, I would like to cite a specific example. Considered by this committee was one of the most hair-brained ideas I have ever heard, and yet it received one first place vote. In contrast, our lunar rendezvous scheme, which I am positive is a much more workable idea, received only bare mention in a negative vein, as was mentioned earlier. Thus, committees are no better than the bias of the men composing them. We might then ask, why are men who are not competent to judge ideas, allowed to judge them?

Perhaps the substance of this section might be summarized this way. Why is NOVA, with its ponderous ideas, whether in size, manufacturing, erection, site location, etc., simply just accepted, and why is a much less grandiose scheme involving rendezvous ostracized or put on the defensive?

PERT chart folly.- When one examines the various program schedules that have been advanced, he cannot help from being impressed by the optimism shown. The remarkable aspect is that the more remote the year, the bolder the schedule becomes. This is, in large measure, due to the PERT chart craze. It has become the vogue to subject practically everything to a PERT chart analysis, whether it means anything or not. Those who apply or make use of it seem to be overcome by a form of self-hypnosis, more or less accepting the point of view, "Because the PERT chart says so, it is so." Somehow, perhaps unfortunately, the year 1967 was mentioned as the target year for putting a man on the moon. The Fleming report through extensive PERT chart analysis then "proved" this could be done. One cannot help but get the feeling that if the year 1966 had been mentioned, then this would have been the date proven; likewise, if 1968 had been the year mentioned.

My quarrel is not with the basic theory of PERT chart analysis; I am fully aware of its usefulness, when properly applied. I have been nominally in charge of a facility development and know the merits, utility, and succinctness by which it is helpful in keeping a going job moving, uncovering bottlenecks, and so forth. But when it is used in the nature of a crystal ball, then I begin to object. Thus, when we scrutinize various schedules and programs, we have to be very careful to ask how realistic the plan really is. Often simple common sense tells us much more than all the machines in the world.

I make the above points because, as you will see, we have a very strong point to make about the possibility of coming up with a realistic schedule; the plan we offer is exceptionally clean and simple in vehicle and booster requirements relative to other plans.

Booster is pacing item.- In working out a paper schedule we have adopted the C-3 development schedule used by Fleming and Heaton, not necessarily because we feel the schedule is realistic, but simply to make a comparison on a parallel basis. But whether the date is right, or not, doesn't matter. Here, I just want to point out that for the lunar rendezvous scheme the C-3 booster is the pacing item. Thus, we can phrase our lunar landing date this way. We can put a man on the moon as soon as the C-3 is developed, and the number of C-3's required is very small. (In fact, as I mentioned earlier, I would not be surprised to have the plan criticized on the basis that it is not grandiose enough.)

Abort.- An item which perhaps deserves special mention is abort. People have leveled criticism, again erroneously and with no knowledge of the situation, that the lunar rendezvous scheme offers no abort possibilities. Along with our many technical studies we have also studied the abort problem quite thoroughly. We find that there is no problem in executing an abort maneuver at any point in the mission. In fact, a very striking result comes out, just the reverse of the impression many people try to create. When one compares, for example, the lunar rendezvous scheme with a direct approach, he finds that on every count the lunar rendezvous method offers a degree of safety and reliability far greater than that possible by the direct approach. These items are touched upon to a limited extent in the attached plan.

Booster Program

My comments on a booster program will be relatively short, since the second attachment more or less speaks for itself. There are, however, a few points worthy of embellishment.

Booster design.- In the course of participating in meetings dealing with vehicle design, I have sometimes had to sit back completely awed and astonished at what I was seeing take place. I have seen the course of an entire meeting change because of an individual not connected with the meeting walking in, looking over shoulders, shaking his head in a negative sense, and then walking out without uttering a word. I have seen people agree on velocity increments, engine performance, and structural data, and after a booster design was made to these figures, have seen some of the people then derate the vehicle simply because they couldn't believe the numbers. I just cannot cater to proceedings of this type. The situation is very much akin to a civil engineer who knows full well that the material he is using will withstand 60,000 psi. He then applies a factor of safety of 2.5, makes a design, then after looking at the results, arbitrarily doubles the size of every member because he isn't quite sure that the design is strong enough. A case in point is the C-3. In my initial contacts with this vehicle, we were assured that it had a payload capability in the neighborhood of 110,000-120,000 lbs. Then it was derated. The value used by the Heaton Committee was 105,000 lbs. By the time the vehicle had reached the Golovin Committee, I was amazed to find that it had a capability of only 82,570 lbs. Perhaps the only comment that can be made to this is that if we can't do any better on making elementary computations of this type, then we deserve to be in the pathetic situation we are. I also wonder where we will stand after NOVA is derated similarly.

"Quantizing" bad.- One of the reasons our booster situation is in such a sad state is the lack of appropriate engines, more specifically the lack of an orderly stepping in engine sizes. Booster progress is virtually at a standstill because there are no engines available, just as engines were the major pacing item in the development of aircraft. Aside from the engines on our smaller boosters, and the H-1 being used on the C-1, the only engines we have in development are:

Capability	Ratio
15,000	
	13.3
200,000	
	7.5
1,500,000	

The attempt to make boosters out of this stock of engines, having very large ratios in capability, can only result in boosters of grotesque and unwieldy configurations, and which require many, many in-flight engine starts. What is needed are engines which step up in size at a lower ratio. Consideration of the staging of an "ideal" rocket system indicates that whether accelerating to orbit speed or to escape speed, the ratio of engine sizes needed is in the order of 3. Logically then we ought to have engines that step in capability by a factor of around 2, 3, or 4. An every-day analog that can be mentioned is outboard motors. There is a motor to serve nearly every need, and in the extreme cases the process of doubling up is even used.

Booster program.- In light of the preceding paragraph, and taking into account the engines under development, we should add the following two:

80,000 - 100,000	$H_2 - O_2$
400,000 - 500,000	$H_2 - O_2$

This would then give a line-up as follows:

15,000	H/O
80,000 - 100,000	H/O
200,000	H/O
400,000 - 500,000	H/O
1,500,000	RP/O

with the 15,000-lb. engine really not needed. This array (plus those mentioned immediately below) would allow the construction of almost all types of boosters conceivable. For example, a single 80,000-100,000 engine would take the place of the six L-115 engines being used on S-IV; not only is the arrangement of six engines on this vehicle bad, but these engines have very poor starting characteristics. The 400,000-500,000 would be used to replace the four J-2's on the S-II. Thus, C-3 would change from a messy 12-engined vehicle requiring 10 in-flight engine starts to a fairly simple 5-engine vehicle with only 3 in-flight engine starts.

In addition, the following engines should be included in a program:

	1,000,000 - 1,500,000 lb.	Solid
	5,000,000	Solid
and/or	5,000,000	Storable

The 1,000,000 - 1,500,000 lb. solid would in itself be a good building block and would probably work in nicely to extend the capabilities of vehicles, such as Titan. The 5,000,000 solid and/or storable would also be good building blocks and specifically would serve as alternate first-stage boosters for C-3, aiming at simplicity and reliability.

It may be said that there is nothing new here and that all of the above is obvious. Indeed, it seems so obvious that one wonders why such a program was not started 5 years ago. But the fact that it may be obvious doesn't help us; what is necessary is putting the obvious into effect. In this connection, there may be some who ask, "But are the plans optimum and the best?". This question is really not pertinent. There will never be an optimized booster or program. We might have an optimum booster for a given situation, but there is none that is optimum for all situations. To seek one, would just cause deliberation to string out indefinitely with little, if any, progress being made. The Dyna-Soar case is a good example of this.

A criticism that undoubtedly will be leveled at the above suggestions is that I'm not being realistic in that there is just not enough money around to do all these things. If this is the situation, then the answer is simply that's why we have Webb and his staff. That's why he was chosen to head the organization, this is one of his major functions, to ask the question, do we want to do a job or not?, and, if so, then to find out where the gaps or holes are, and then to go about doing what is necessary to fill the gaps to make sure the job gets done, Further, the load doesn't have to be carried by the NASA alone. The Air Force and NASA can work together and share the load, and I'm sure that if this is done, the necessary money can be found. Even if some project, say, for example, the 5,000,000-lb. storable engine has to be dropped for some reason after it gets started; no harm will be done. This happens every day. On the contrary, some good, some new knowledge, will have been uncovered, even if it turns out to be the discovery of the next obstacle which prevents such a booster from being built.

Nuclear booster and booster size.- Although not mentioned in the previous section, work on nuclear engines should, of course, continue. Any progress made here will integrate very nicely into the booster plans indicated in the attachment.

As regards booster size, the following comment is offered. Excluding for the moment NOVA type vehicles, we should strive for boosters which make use of the engines mentioned in the preceding section and which are the biggest that can be made and yet still be commensurate with existing test-stand sites and with the use of launch sites that are composed of an array of assembly buildings and multiple launch pads. The idea behind launch sites of this type is an excellent one. It keeps real estate demands to a minimum, allows for ease in vehicle assembly and check-out, and greatly eases the launch rate problem. Thus, C-3 or C-4 should be designed accordingly. We would then have a nice work-horse type vehicle having relative ease of handling, and which would permit a lunar landing mission, as indicated earlier in the lunar rendezvous write-up section. From my point of view, I would much rather confine my spending to a single versatile launch site of the type mentioned, save money in real estate acquisition and launch site development necessary for the huge vehicles, and put the money saved into an engine development program.

Concluding Remarks

It is one thing to gripe, another to offer constructive criticism. Thus, in making a few final remarks I would like to offer what I feel would be a sound integrated overall program. I think we should:

1. Get a manned rendezvous experiment going with the Mark II Mercury.

2. Firm up the engine program suggested in this letter and attachment, converting the booster to these engines as soon as possible.

3. Establish the concept of using a C-3 and lunar rendezvous to accomplish the manned lunar landing as a firm program.

Naturally, in discussing matters of the type touched upon herein, one cannot make comments without having them smack somewhat against NOVA. I want to assure you, however, I'm not trying to say NOVA should not be built. I'm simply trying to establish that our scheme deserves a parallel front-line position. As a matter of fact, because the lunar rendezvous approach is easier, quicker, less costly, requires less development, less new sites and facilities, it would appear more appropriate to say that this is the way to go, and that we will use NOVA as a follow on. Give us the go-ahead, and a C-3, and we will put men on the moon in very short order - and we don't need any Houston empire to do it.

In closing, Dr. Seamans, let me say that should you desire to discuss the points covered in this letter in more detail, I would welcome the opportunity to come up to Headquarters to discuss them with you.

Respectfully yours,

John C. Houbolt

JCH.fbm

Encls.

CONCLUDING REMARKS BY DR. WERNHER VON BRAUN
ABOUT MODE SELECTION FOR THE LUNAR LANDING PROGRAM
GIVEN TO DR. JOSEPH F. SHEA, DEPUTY DIRECTOR (SYSTEMS)
OFFICE OF MANNED SPACE FLIGHT
JUNE 7, 1962

In the previous six hours we presented to you the results of some of the many studies we at Marshall have prepared in connection with the Manned Lunar Landing Project. The purpose of all these studies was to identify potential technical problem areas, and to make sound and realistic scheduling estimates. All studies were aimed at assisting you in your final recommendation with respect to the mode to be chosen for the Manned Lunar Landing Project.

Our general conclusion is that all four modes investigated are technically feasible and could be implemented with enough time and money. We have, however, arrived at a definite list of preferences in the following order:

1. Lunar Orbit Rendezvous Mode - with the strong recommendation (to make up for the limited growth potential of this mode) to initiate, simultaneously, the development of an unmanned, fully automatic, one-way C-5 logistics vehicle.

2. Earth Orbit Rendezvous Mode (Tanking Mode).

3. C-5 Direct Mode with minimum size Command Module and High Energy Return.

4. Nova or C-8 Mode.

I shall give you the reasons behind this conclusion in just one minut

But first I would like to reiterate once more that it is absolutely mandatory that we arrive at a definite mode decision within the next few weeks, preferably by the first of July, 1962. We are already losing tim in our over-all program as a result of a lacking mode decision.

CLASSIFICATION CHANGE
To Unclassified
By authority of [illegible] SCD-4, 5/1/70 + SCD-11, 7/1/70 signed by Jacob E. Smart
Changed by [illegible] Date 8/28/70

A typical example is the S-IVB contract. If the S-IVB stage is to serve not only as the third (escape) stage for the C-5, but also as the second stage for the C-1B needed in support of rendezvous tests, a flyable S-IVB will be needed at least one year earlier than if there was no C-1B at all. The impact of this question on facility planning, build-up of contractor level of effort, etc., should be obvious.

Furthermore, if we do not freeze the mode now, we cannot lay out a definite program with a schedule on which the budgets for FY-1964 and following can be based. Finally, if we do not make a clear-cut decision on the mode very soon, our chances of accomplishing the first lunar expedition in this decade will fade away rapidly.

WHY DO WE RECOMMEND LUNAR ORBIT RENDEZVOUS MODE PLUS C-5 ONE-WAY LOGISTICS VEHICLE?

a. We believe this program offers the highest confidence factor of successful accomplishment within this decade.

b. It offers an adequate performance margin. With storable propellants, both for the Service Module and Lunar Excursion Module, we should have a comfortable padding with respect to propulsion performance and weights. The performance margin could be further increased by initiation of a back-up development aimed at a High Energy Propulsion System for the Service Module and possibly the Lunar Excursion Module. Additional performance gains could be obtained if current proposals by Rocketdyne to increase the thrust and/or specific impulses of the F-1 and J-2 engines were implemented.

c. We agree with the Manned Spacecraft Center that the designs of a maneuverable hyperbolic re-entry vehicle and of a lunar landing vehicle constitute the two most critical tasks in producing a successful lunar spacecraft. A drastic separation of these two functions into two separate elements is bound to greatly simplify the development of the spacecraft system. Developmental cross-feed between results from simulated or actual landing tests, on the one hand, and re-entry tests, on the other, are minimized if no attempt is made to include the Command Module into the lunar landing process. The mechanical separation of the two functions would virtually permit completely parallel developments of the Command Module and the Lunar Excursion Module. While it may be difficult to accurately appraise this advantage in terms of months to be gained, we have no doubt whatsoever that such a procedure will indeed result in very substantial saving of time.

d. We believe that the combination of the Lunar Orbit Rendezvous Mode and a C-5 one-way Logistics Vehicle offers a great growth potential. After the first successful landing on the moon, demands for follow-on programs will essentially center on increased lunar surface mobility and increased material supplies for shelter, food, oxygen, scientific instrumentation, etc. It appears that the Lunar Excursion Module, when refilled with propellants brought down by the Logistics Vehicle, constitutes an ideal means for lunar surface transportation. First estimates indicate that in the 1/6 G gravitational field of the moon, the Lunar Excursion Module, when used as a lunar taxi, would have a radius of action of at least 40 miles from around the landing point of the Logistics Vehicle. It may well be that on the rocky and treacherous lunar terrain the Lunar Excursion Module will turn out to be a far more attractive type of a taxi than a wheeled or caterpillar vehicle.

e. We believe the Lunar Orbit Rendezvous Mode using a single C-5 offers a very good chance of ultimately growing into a C-5 direct capability. At this time we recommend against relying on the C-5 Direct Mode because of its need for a much lighter command module as well as a high energy landing and return propulsion system. While it may be unwise to count on the availability of such advanced equipment during this decade (this is why this mode was given a number 3 rating) it appears entirely within reach in the long haul.

f. If and when at some later time a reliable nuclear third stage for Saturn C-5 emerges from the RIFT program, the performance margin for the C-5 Direct Mode will become quite comfortable.

g. Conversely, if the Advanced Saturn C-5 were dropped in favor of a Nova or C-8, it would completely upset all present plans for the implementation of the RIFT program. Contracts, both for the engines and the RIFT stage, have already been let and would probably have to be cancelled until a new program could be developed.

h. We conclude from our studies that an automatic pinpoint letdown on the lunar surface going through a circumlunar orbit and using a landing beacon is entirely possible. Whether this method should be limited to the C-5 Logistics Vehicle or be adopted as a secondary mode for the Lunar Excursion Module is a matter that should be carefully discussed with the Manned Spacecraft Center. It may well be that the demand for incorporation of an additional automatic landing capability in the Lunar Excursion Module buys more trouble than gains.

i. The Lunar Orbit Rendezvous Mode augmented by a C-5 Logistics Vehicle undoubtedly offers the cleanest managerial interfaces between the Manned Spacecraft Center, Marshall Space Flight Center, Launch Operations Center and all our contractors. While the precise effect of this may be hard to appraise, it is a commonly accepted fact that the number and the nature of technical and managerial interfaces are very major factors in conducting a complex program on a tight time schedule. There are already a frightening number of interfaces in existence in our Manned Lunar Landing Program. There are interfaces between the stages of the launch vehicles, between launch vehicles and spacecraft, between complete space vehicles and their ground equipment, between manned and automatic checkout, and in the managerial area between the Centers, the Washington Program Office, and the contractors. The plain result of too many interfaces is a continuous and disastrous erosion of the authority vested in the line organization and the need for more coordination meetings, integration groups, working panels, ad-hoc committees, etc. Every effort should therefore be made to reduce the number of technical and managerial interfaces to a bare minimum.

j. Compared with the C-5 Direct Mode or the Nova/C-8 Mode, the Lunar Orbit Rendezvous Mode offers the advantage that no existing contracts for stages (if we go to Nova) or spacecraft systems (if we go to C-5 Direct) have to be terminated; that the contractor structure in existence can be retained; that the contract negotiations presently going on can be finished under the existing set of ground rules; that the contractor build-up program (already in full swing) can be continued as planned; that facilities already authorized and under construction can be built as planned, etc.

k. We at the Marshall Space Flight Center readily admit that when first exposed to the proposal of the Lunar Orbit Rendezvous Mode we were a bit skeptical - particularly of the aspect of having the astronauts execute a complicated rendezvous maneuver at a distance of 240,000 miles from the earth where any rescue possibility appeared remote. In the meantime, however, we have spent a great deal of time and effort studying the four modes, and we have come to the conclusion that this particular disadvantage is far outweighed by the advantages listed above.

We understand that the Manned Spacecraft Center was also quite skeptical at first when John Houbolt of Langley advanced the proposal of the Lunar Orbit Rendezvous Mode, and that it took them quite a while to substantiate the feasibility of the method and finally endorse it.

Against this background it can, therefore, be concluded that the issue of "invented here" versus "not invented here" does not apply to either the Manned Spacecraft Center or the Marshall Space Flight Center; that both Centers have actually embraced a scheme suggested by a third source. Undoubtedly, personnel of MSC and MSFC have by now conducted more detailed studies on all aspects of the four modes than any other group. Moreover, it is these two Centers to which the Office of Manned Space Flight would ultimately have to look to "deliver the goods". I consider it fortunate indeed for the Manned Lunar Landing Program that both Centers, after much soul searching, have come to identical conclusions. This should give the Office of Manned Space Flight some additional assurance that our recommendations should not be too far from the truth.

II. WHY DO WE NOT RECOMMEND THE EARTH ORBIT RENDEZVOUS MODE?

Let me point out again that we at the Marshall Space Flight Center consider the Earth Orbit Rendezvous Mode entirely feasible. Specifically, we found the Tanking Mode substantially superior to the Connecting Mode. Compared to the Lunar Orbit Rendezvous Mode, it even seems to offer a somewhat greater performance margin. This is true even if only the nominal two C-5's (tanker and manned lunar vehicle) are involved, but the performance margin could be further enlarged almost indefinitely by the use of additional tankers.

We have spent more time and effort here at Marshall on studies of the Earth Orbit Rendezvous Mode (Tanking and Connecting Modes) than on any other mode. This is attested to by six big volumes describing all aspects of this mode. Nor do we think that in the light of our final recommendation - to adopt the Lunar Orbit Rendezvous Mode instead - this effort was in vain. Earth Orbit Rendezvous as a general operational procedure will undoubtedly play a major role in our over-all national space flight program, and the use of it is even mandatory in developing a Lunar Orbit Rendezvous capability.

The reasons why, in spite of these advantages, we moved it down to position number 2 on our totem pole are as follows:

a. We consider the Earth Orbit Rendezvous Mode more complex and costlier than Lunar Orbit Rendezvous. Moreover, lunar mission success with Earth Orbit Rendezvous requires two consecutive successful launches. If, for example, after a successful tanker launch, the manned lunar vehicle aborts during its ascent, or fails to get off the pad within a certain permissible period of time, the first (tanker) flight must also be written off as useless for the mission.

b. The interface problems arising between the Manned Spacecraft Center and the Marshall Space Flight Center, both in the technical and management areas, would be more difficult if the Earth Orbit Rendezvous Mode was adopted. For example, if the tanker as an unmanned vehicle was handled by MSFC, and the flight of the manned lunar vehicle was conducted by the Manned Spacecraft Center, a managerial interface arises between target and chaser. On the other hand, if any one of the two Centers would take over the entire mission, it would probably bite off more than it could chew, with the result of even more difficult and unpleasant interface problems.

c. According to repeated statements by Bob Gilruth, the Apollo Command Module in its presently envisioned form is simply unsuited for lunar landing because of the poor visibility conditions and the undesirable supine position of the astronauts during landing.

III. WHY DO WE NOT RECOMMEND THE C-5 DIRECT MODE?

It is our conviction that the C-5 Direct Mode will ultimately become feasible - once we know more about hyperbolic re-entry, and once we have adequate high energy propulsion systems available that can be used conveniently and reliably on the surface of the moon. With the advent of a nuclear third stage for C-5, the margin for this capability will be substantially widened, of course.

a. Our main reason against recommending the C-5 Direct Mode is its marginal weight allowance for the spacecraft and the demand for high energy return propulsion, combined with the time factor, all of which would impose a very substantial additional burden on the Manned Spacecraft Center.

b. The Manned Spacecraft Center has spent a great deal of time and effort in determining realistic spacecraft weights. In the opinion of Bob Gilruth and Chuck Mathews, it would simply not be realistic to expect that a lunar spacecraft light enough to be used with the C-5 Direct Mode could be developed during this decade with an adequate degree of confidence.

c. The demand for a high energy return propulsion system, which is implicit in the C-5 Direct Mode, is considered undesirable by the Manned Spacecraft Center - at the present state-of-the-art at least - because this propulsion system must also double up as an extra-atmospheric abort propulsion system. For this purpose, MSC considers a propulsion system as simple and reliable as possible (storable and hypergolic propellants) as absolutely mandatory. We think the question of inherent reliability of storable versus high energy propulsion systems - and their usability in the lunar surface environment - can be argued, but as long as the requirement for "storables" stands, the C-5 Direct Mode is not feasible performance-wise.

d. NASA has already been saddled with one program (Centaur) where the margin between performance claims for launch vehicle and demands for payload weights were drawn too closely. We do not consider it prudent to repeat this mistake.

IV. WHY DO WE RECOMMEND AGAINST THE NOVA OR C-8 MODE?

It should be clearly understood that our recommendation against the Nova or C-8 Mode at this time refers solely to its use as a launch vehicle for the implementation of the President's commitment to put a man on the moon in this decade. We at Marshall feel very strongly that the Advanced Saturn C-5 is not the end of the line as far as major launch vehicles are concerned! Undoubtedly, as we shall be going about setting up a base on the moon and beginning with the manned exploration of the planets, there will be a great need for launch vehicles more powerful than the C-5. But for these purposes such a new vehicle could be conceived and developed on a more relaxed time schedule. It would be a true follow-on launch vehicle. All of our studies aimed at NASA's needs for a true manned interplanetary capability indicate that a launch vehicle substantially more powerful than one powered by eight F-1 engines would be required. Our recommendation, therefore, should be formulated as follows: "Let us take Nova or C-8 out of the race of putting an American on the moon in this decade, but let us develop a sound concept for a follow-on 'Supernova' launch vehicle".

Here are our reasons for recommending to take Nova or C-8 out of the present Manned Lunar Landing Program:

a. As previously stated, the Apollo system in its present form is not landable on the moon. The spacecraft system would require substantial changes from the presently conceived configuration. The same argument is, of course, applicable to the Earth Orbit Rendezvous Mode.

b. With the S-II stage of the Advanced Saturn C-5 serving as a second stage of a C-8 (boosted by eight F-1 engines) we would have an undesirable, poorly staged, hybrid launch vehicle, with a payload capability far below the maximum obtainable with the same first stage. Performance-wise, with its escape capability of only 132,000 lbs. (in lieu of the 150,000 lbs. demanded) it would still be too marginal, without a high energy return propulsion system, to land the present Apollo Command Module on the surface of the moon.

c. Implementation of the Nova or C-8 program in addition to the Advanced Saturn C-5 would lead to two grossly underfunded and under-managed programs with resulting abject failure of both. Implementation of the Nova or C-8 program in lieu of the Advanced Saturn C-5 would have an absolutely disastrous impact on all our facility plans.

The rafter height of the Michoud plant is 40 feet. The diameter of the S-IC is 33 feet. As a result, most of the assembly operations for the S-IC booster of the C-5 can take place in a horizontal position. Only a relatively narrow high bay tower must be added to the main building for a few operations which must be carried out in a vertical position. A Nova or C-8 booster, however, has a diameter of approximately 50 feet. This means that the roof of a very substantial portion of the Michoud plant would have to be raised by 15 to 20 feet. Another alternative would be to build a very large high bay area where every operation involving cumbersome parts would be done in a vertical position. In either case the very serious question arises whether under these circumstances the Michoud plant was a good selection to begin with.

The foundation situation at Michoud is so poor that extensive pile driving is necessary. This did not bother us when we acquired the plant because the many thousands of piles on which it rests were driven twenty years ago by somebody else. But if we had to enter into a major pile driving operation now, the question would immediately arise as to whether we could not find other building sites where foundations could be prepared cheaper and faster.

Any tampering with the NASA commitment to utilize the Michoud plant, however, would also affect Chrysler's S-1 program, for which tooling and plant preparation are already in full swing at Michoud. Raising the roof and driving thousands of piles in Michoud may turn out to be impossible while Chrysler is assembling S-I's in the same hangar.

In summary, the impact of a switch from C-5 to Nova/C-8 on the very concept of Michoud, would call for a careful and detailed study whose outcome with respect to continued desirability of the use of the Michoud plant appears quite doubtful. We consider it most likely that discontinuance of the C-5 plan in favor of Nova or C-8 would reopen the entire Michoud decision and would throw the entire program into turmoil with ensuing unpredictable delays. The construction of a new plant would take at least 2-1/2 years to beneficial occupancy and over 3 years to start of production.

d. At the Marshall Space Flight Center, construction of a static test stand for S-IC booster is well under way. In its present form this test stand cannot be used for the first stage of Nova or C-8. Studies indicate that as far as the noise level is concerned, there will probably be no objection to firing up eight F-1 engines at MSFC. However, the Marshall test stand construction program would be greatly delayed, regardless of what approach we would take to accommodate Nova/C-8 stages. Detailed studies seem to indicate that the fastest course of action, if Nova or C-8 were adopted, would be to build

- a brand new eight F-1 booster test stand south of the present S-IC test stand, and

- convert the present S-IC test stand into an N-II test stand. (This latter conclusion is arrived at because the firing of an N-II stage at Santa Susanna is not possible for safety reasons, the S-II propellant load being considered the absolute maximum permissible.)

The Mississippi Test Facility is still a "cow pasture that NASA doesn't even own yet", and cannot compete with any test stand availability dates in Huntsville. Developments of basic utilities (roads, water, power, sewage, canals, rail spur, etc.) at MTF will require well over a year, and all scheduling studies indicate that whatever we build at MTF is about 18 months behind comparable facilities built in Huntsville. MTF should, therefore, be considered an acceptance firing and product improvement site for Michoud products rather than a basic development site.

e. In view of the fact that the S-II stage is not powerful enough for the Apollo direct flight mission profile, a second stage powered by eight or nine J-2's or two M-1's is needed. Such a stage would again be on the order of 40 to 50 feet in diameter. No studies have been made as to whether it could be built in the Downey/Seal Beach complex. It is certain, however, that its static testing in Santa Susanna is impossible. As a result, we would have to take an entirely new look at the NAA contract.

f. I have already mentioned the disruptive effect a cancellation of the C-5 would have on the RIFT program.

g. One of the strongest arguments against replacement of the Advanced Saturn C-5 by Nova or C-8 is that such a decision would topple our entire contractor structure. It should be remembered that the temporary uncertainty about the relatively minor question of whether NAA should assemble at Seal Beach or Eglin cost us a delay of almost half a year. I think it should not take much imagination to realize what would happen if we were to tell Boeing, NAA and Douglas that the C-5 was out; that we are going to build a booster with eight F-1 engines, a second stage with eight or nine J-2's or maybe two M-1 engines; and that the entire problem of manufacturing and testing facilities must be re-evaluated.

We already have several thousands of men actually at work on these three stages and many of them have been dislocated from their home plants in implementation of our present C-5 program. Rather than leaving these thousands of men suspended (although supported by NASA dollars) in a state of uncertainty over an extended period of new systems analysis, program implementation studies, budget reshuffles, site selection procedures, etc., it may indeed turn out to be wiser to just terminate the existing contracts and advise the contractors that we will call them back once we have a new program plan laid out for them. We have no doubt that the termination costs incurring to NASA by doing this would easily amount to several hundred million dollars.

I have asked a selected group of key Marshall executives for their appraisal, in terms of delay of the first orbital launch, if the C-5 was to be discontinued and replaced by a Nova or C-8. The estimates of these men (whose duties it would be to implement the new program) varied between 14 and 24 months with an <u>average</u> estimate of an over-all delay of <u>19 months</u>.

h. In appraising the total loss to NASA, it should also not be overlooked that we are supporting engine development teams at various contractor plants at the rate of many tens of millions of dollars per year for every stage of C-1 and C-5. If the exact definition of the stages were delayed by switching to Nova/C-8, these engine development teams would have to be held on the NASA payroll for just that much longer, in order to assure proper engine/stage integration.

i. More than twelve months of past extensive effort at the Marshall Space Flight Center to analyze and define the Advanced Saturn C-5 system in a great deal of engineering detail would have to be written off as a flat loss, if we abandoned the C-5 now. This item alone, aside from the time irretrievably lost, represents an expenditure of over one hundred million dollars.

j. The unavoidable uncertainty in many areas created by a switch to Nova or C-8 (Can we retain present C-5 contractors? Where are the new fabrication sites? Where are we going to static test? etc.) may easily lead to delays even well in excess of the estimates given above. For in view of the political pressures invariably exerted on NASA in connection with facility siting decisions, it is quite likely that even the NASA Administrator himself will find himself frequently unable to make binding decisions without demanding from OMSF an extensive re-appraisal of a multitude of issues related with siting. There was ample evidence of this during the past year.

k. For all the reasons quoted above, the Marshall Space Flight Center considers a discontinuation of the Advanced Saturn C-5 in favor of Nova or C-8 as the <u>worst</u> of the four proposed modes for implementation of the manned lunar landing project. <u>We at Marshall would consider a decision in favor of this mode to be tantamount with giving up the race to put a man on the moon in this decade even before we started.</u>

IN SUMMARY I THEREFORE RECOMMEND THAT:

a. The Lunar Orbit Rendezvous Mode be adopted.

b. A development of an unmanned, fully automatic, one-way C-5 Logistics Vehicle be undertaken in support of the lunar expedition.

c. The C-1 program as established today be retained and that, in accordance with progress made in S-IVB development, the C-1 be gradually replaced by the C-1B.

d. A C-1B program be officially established and approved with adequate funding.

e. The development of high energy propulsion systems be initiated as a back-up for the Service Module and possibly the Lunar Excursion Module.

f. Supplements to present development contracts to Rocketdyne on the F-1 and J-2 engines be let to increase thrust and/or specific impulse.

Wernher von Braun, Director
George C. Marshall Space Flight Center

**The Road to the Lunar-Orbit Rendezvous Decision:
Presentations by John C. Houbolt**

Date	Location	Committee/Audience
Sept. 1959	Langley Research Center	Manned Space Laboratory Group
Dec. 1959	Langley Research Center	Goett Committee
Feb. 1960	Langley Research Center	Manned Space Laboratory Group
Apr. 1960	New York City	Society of Automotive Engineers
Spring 1960	Langley Research Center	Robert Piland and Space Task Group Members
Spring 1960	Langley Research Center	William Mrazek
May 1960	Langley Research Center	Intercenter Review
Sept. 1960	Langley Research Center	Robert C. Seamans, Jr.
Nov. 1960	The Pentagon	Air Force Scientific Advisory Board
Dec. 1960	Langley Research Center	Space Task Group Leaders
Dec. 1960	NASA Headquarters	Headquarters Staff (Glennan, von Braun, Seamans, and Faget)
Jan. 1961	NASA Headquarters	Space Exploration Program Council
Jan. 1961	Langley Research Center	Space Task Group Members
Jan. 1961	Langley Research Center	Low Committee Representative
Jan. 1961	NASA Headquarters	NASA Headquarters Staff
Apr. 1961	Langley Research Center	Space Task Group
May 1961		First Letter to Seamans
Jun. 1961	NASA Headquarters	Lundin Committee
Jun. 1961	France	International Space Flight Symposium

Jul. 1961	Langley Research Center	Rehearsal with Space Task Group
Jul. 1961	Washington, DC	NASA/Industry Apollo Technical Conference
Aug. 1961	NASA Headquarters	Golovin Committee
Aug. 1961	Langley Research Center	Space Task Group
Nov. 1961		Second Letter to Seamans
Jan. 1962	Langley Research Center	Joseph Shea and Space Task Group
Jan. 1962	Houston, TX	Manned Spacecraft Center Personnel
Feb. 1962	NASA Headquarters	Manned Space Flight Management Council
Apr. 1962		Report and papers sent to Wernher von Braun
Jun. 1962	Marshall Space Flight Center	Lunar Mode Decision Conference

About the Author

James R. Hansen is Professor of History at Auburn University in Auburn, Alabama. He is the author of several books, articles, and reviews in aerospace history and the history of technology, including *Engineer in Charge: A History of the Langley Aeronautical Laboratory, 1917–1958* (NASA Special Publication-4305, 1987); *From the Ground Up: The Autobiography of an Aeronautical Engineer* (Smithsonian Institution Press, 1988), coauthored by American aviation pioneer Fred E. Weick; and *Spaceflight Revolution: NASA Langley Research Center from Sputnik to Apollo* (NASA Special version of this study. At Auburn University, Dr. Hansen teaches courses on the history of flight, the history of science, and space history, as well as a large auditorium class that surveys the history of technology from ancient times to the present. Dr. Hansen earned an A.B. degree, with high honors, from Indiana University (1974) and an M.A. (1976) and Ph.D. (1981) from The Ohio State University.

Monographs in Aerospace History

Launius, Roger D. and Gillette, Aaron K., compilers. *Toward a History of the Space Shuttle: An Annotated Bibliography* (Monographs in Aerospace History, No. 1, 1992).

Launius, Roger D., and Hunley, J.D., compilers. *An Annotated Bibliography of the Apollo Program* (Monographs in Aerospace History, No. 2, 1994).

Launius, Roger D. *Apollo: A Retrospective Analysis* (Monographs in Aerospace History, No. 3, 1994).

Hansen, James R. *Enchanted Rendezvous: John C. Houbolt and the Genesis of the Lunar-Orbit Rendezvous Concept* (Monographs in Aerospace History, No. 4, 1995, reprinted 1999).

Gorn, Michael H. *Hugh L. Dryden's Career in Aviation and Space* (Monographs in Aerospace History, No. 5, 1996).

Powers, Sheryll Goecke. *Women in Flight Research at NASA Dryden Flight Research Center from 1946 to 1995* (Monographs in Aerospace History, No. 6, 1997).

Portree, David S.F. and Trevino, Robert C. *Walking to Olympus: An EVA Chronology* (Monographs in Aerospace History, No. 7, 1997).

Logsdon, John M., moderator. *Legislative Origins of the National Aeronautics and Space Act of 1958: Proceedings of an Oral History Workshop* (Monographs in Aerospace History, No. 8, 1998).

Rumerman, Judy A., compiler. *U.S. Human Spaceflight, A Record of Achievement 1961-1998* (Monographs in Aerospace History, No. 9, 1998).

Portree, David S. F. *NASA's Origins and the Dawn of the Space Age* (Monographs in Aerospace History, No. 10, 1998).

Logsdon, John M. *Together in Orbit: The Origins of International Cooperation in the Space Station* (Monographs in Aerospace History, No. 11, 1998).

Phillips, W. Hewitt. *Journey in Aeronautical Research: A Career at NASA Langley Research Center* (Monographs in Aerospace History, No. 12, 1998).

www.ingramcontent.com/pod-product-compliance
Lightning Source LLC
Chambersburg PA
CBHW081237090426
42738CB00016B/3344
* 9 7 8 1 7 8 0 3 9 3 1 4 8 *